The Year of Dangerously Designing

ALSO BY ADAM D. CARFAGNO CHERSON

Non-Fiction: Environmental Science, Law, and Policy

Ecocide: Environmental Gloom and Doom Explained in Everyday Language

Political Ecologies: Essays in Environmental Science and Policy

Marine Debris: A Policy Analysis (co-author)

Eutrophication in the Metropolitan Hudson River Estuary (co-author)

Pro-Environmental Behavior of Public and Private Management Students (co-author)

Addressing Electronic Waste in New York City (co-author)

Non-Fiction: Philology

Lucubrations From the Labyrinth of Arts and Letters

The Literary Imagination Under Totalitarian Regimes: A Cuban Case Study

Lo Latino en el Arte (editor)

Fiction, Poetry, Drama, Opera, and Film

Scrypts: Libretti, Film Scripts, and Animation Scripts

Hearts Were Broken in the Museum of Unusable Things

The Year of Dangerously Designing

From Environmental Theory to Social Entrepreneurship

Adam D. Carfagno Cherson

Doctor of Jurisprudence
Master of Public Administration

Greencore Books
New York

The Year of Dangerously Designing

ISBN: 978-1-520-63392-3

Published in the United States of America

Cover Image: Artist's rendering of the Carbon Sequestration and Storage Infrastructure described in Chapter 1 overlaid by a detailed process flow diagram of the same technology

For Father and Mother, For Imbuing Me with the Spirits of Futurism and Humanism

Contents

INTRODUCTION

After many rewarding years of critical thinking, research, and analysis on environmental themes, for the past year or so I have worked to transfer my theoretical environmentalism into the real-world domain. Instead of simply describing adverse environmental impacts and problems I have sought to propose actual techniques and technologies that could lead to a more environmentally sustainable future. The result is the ten projects presented here. They exemplify the heroic and possible quixotic effort of a social scientist to become a social entrepreneur. These projects provide answers to the question: 'well, supposing you are right, what can we do about our environmental woes anyhow?' Passing from theory into practice is a potentially dangerous undertaking due to the very real possibilities of financial, professional, and legal ruin. It can also be exhilarating and just plain fun too— whether or not an angel investor, think tank, incubator, or precocious protégé elevates any of these products or techniques to the next level of development.

INFRASTRUCTURE FOR A CHANGING WORLD

Project: Sustainable Global Change Infrastructure

Entrepreneurial Platform(s): Virgin Earth Challenge; National Science Foundation's Environmental Sustainability Program; The Economist of London's Challenge on the Capture of Atmospheric Carbon to Address Global Warming; Journal of Environmental Engineering; Columbia University Technology Ventures; Mohr Davidow Ventures; Wordpress; Google Sketchup

Submitted: 9/8/2010 and thereafter

Background

The original concept arose from the realization that the Kyoto Protocol would most likely fail to meet its targets and that international cooperation on climate change abatement would probably take too long to have any impact. The obvious strategy based on these realities is atmospheric carbon capture and re-use or storage. I decided to design a system and process that could be implemented today by a smaller group of industrialized nations and that would have a significant global impact towards curtailing climate change. I made it an essential feature to integrate economic and social constraints and requirements into the plan. Not only would the science have to work, but the system would need to be politically and economically feasible. Thus was born the Sustainable Global Change Infrastructure, a system for carbon capture, economic use, and storage. After obtaining patent protection, I made use of the then brand-spanking-new LinkedIn to gather together world renowned experts in the various fields to present the concept for funding. This was some of the most interesting and exciting environmental work I have ever done. The following description consists of the executive summary submitted to venture capital firms, followed by the Virgin Earth Challenge cover letter addressing the challenge criteria, and then the detailed proposal submitted to the Economist Challenge (including figures).

AQUASEQ TECHNOLOGY

Executive Summary[1]

The development of carbon capture and storage methods and the underlying problem of global geochemical and climate change been identified by many eminent thinkers and prestigious institutions as one of the grandest challenges for humanity in the 21st Century. The goal of this venture is the near-term commercialization of a sustainable atmospheric carbon capture and storage system (the 'AquaSeq Technology'). The product development and advisory team consists of some of the world's leading experts and practitioners in their various fields of endeavor. The salient features and benefits of the AquaSeq Technology are exemplified in the following diagram:

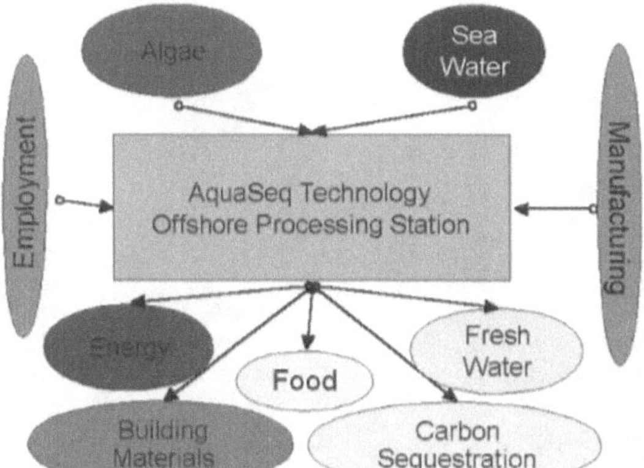

Description of Technology

The competitive advantage of the AquaSeq Technology resides in: 1) its provision of essential products and services from an offshore position where the needed natural resources and space abound, and 2) its unification of the four major steps of atmospheric carbon removal (capture, separation, transformation, and sequestration) into one continuous and self-contained operational process, potentially solving many engineering challenges to large-scale greenhouse gas mitigation. The system combines offshore algae farming and biomass pyrolysis with syngas production and brine creation to drive a chemical process of bicarbonate and ammonium production--- all supported financially by a set of sustainable co-products and co-services. An artist's conception of the system shows a seaweed cultivation area feeding into a floating processing station:

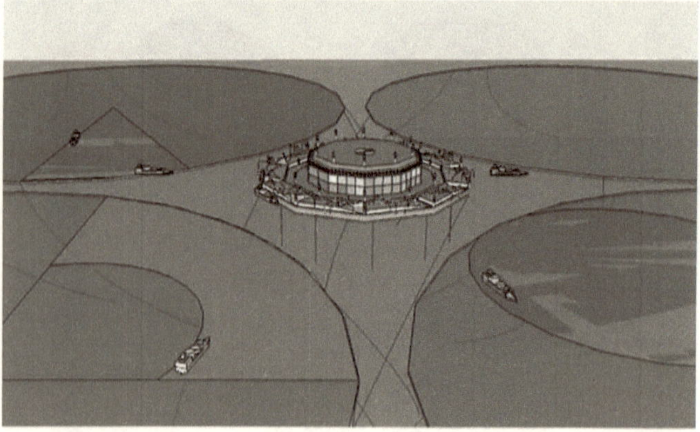

A fully explorable, 3D computer assisted design version of this graphic for the Google Sketchup platform is available here for download: http://image.xyvy.info/AquaSeq.skp

Commercial Viability

The market sector occupied by the AquaSeq Technology is roughly described as the clean tech infrastructure sector. Within this sector, the market niches can be further defined as clean water, green building materials, and fertilizer production, solid waste disposal, and carbon mitigation. Each of these sub-sectors, with the possible exception of the last, is certain to grow far into the future due to population and economic growth pressures throughout the world. The future course of the carbon mitigation market is largely dependent on policy determinations that are still in a state of flux. The AquaSeq Technology is commercially sustainable whether or not the future provides a robust carbon market or not and its deployment will lead to significant amounts of industrial and economic activity of benefit to nations at all stages of development.

Research and Development Team

Clifford Goudey, ME, has over 30 years of experience in developing technologies for working on and under the ocean. A consistent theme of his work has been the introduction of innovative ways of tapping the productivity of the ocean in more sustainable ways. Much of this career has been as a research engineer at the Massachusetts Institute of Technology, where he was Director of the Offshore Aquaculture Engineering Center for 11 years.

Dennis Hanisak, PhD, Director of the Center for Marine Ecosystem Health at the Harbor Branch Oceanographic Institute, has 30 years of experience in marine biology and ecology, with emphasis on marine plants, particularly macroalgae (seaweeds) and seagrasses and the use of seaweeds for carbon capture. Dr. Hanisak is the author of over 70 scientific publications, a frequently invited participant at national and international meetings and workshops, a past President of the International Phycological Society, and a past President and Chairman of the Board of Trustees of the Phycological Society of America.

Marco Castaldi, PhD, is the Director of the Combustion and Catalysis Lab at Columbia University. He has had extensive experience in using stable intermediates to successfully determine the mechanisms of polycyclic aromatic hydrocarbon (PAH) formation from simple fuels, to logistical fuel catalytic reforming, to water gas shift reactions. By accurately measuring only the stable intermediates that were produced in various zones of the flame, it enabled a very thorough understanding the various reaction pathways that produced PAH's thus bridging the gap in understanding from gaseous reactants to soot particle formation. That methodology will be used here with the expectation that new intermediates or low concentration products not previously measured will significantly contribute to understanding the mechanisms governing those processes.

Ken Rollins, FIChemE, has achieved the highest ranking, Fellow of the Institution, given by the Institution of Chemical Engineers in recognition of his 40 years of chemical engineering experience. His 18 years as a Senior Chemical Engineer at Jacobs Engineering and 7 years as Senior Process Engineer at Costain, among other assignments, have involved work with fine chemicals, pharmaceuticals, energy, waste treatment, emission control, fertilizers and many other processes and projects, including combustion engineering and nuclear reprocessing. Representative projects over the years have included the management of suites of small projects as well as taking a leadership role in larger ones. He has a thorough knowledge of process safety analysis techniques. He is also an experienced commissioning engineer and technical writer. His current professional interests have turned to the development of the worldwide biomass utilization industry, including white biotechnology routes to platform chemicals and the creation of biodegradable materials from non-food biomass feedstocks.

Xinping Hu, PhD, is a post-doctoral researcher at the University of Georgia's Department of Marine

Sciences. He has extensive knowledge and research experiences in both coastal carbon studies and pelagic oceanography. Dr. Hu has participated in collaborative studies that examine carbon fluxes in ocean margins and river-ocean interactions and published papers in both ocean/sediment biogeochemistry and intrusion of anthropogenic CO_2 into oceanic environments.

Dale Kiefer, PhD, is the Director of the Kiefer Lab at the University of Southern California, specializing in marine GIS. Through his firm, System Science Applications, he provides expertise in at-sea monitoring as well as bio-optical and planktonic algorithm development for implementation within the EASy GIS software. He is a former member of the SeaWiFs Science team of NASA and early developer of algorithms for remote sensing of ocean color and photosynthesis. His particular specialty involves the application of remote sensing to such problems. He has published over 50 papers, which most often explore the fields of marine microbiology and optics. He has also obtained 3 United States patents for inventions in optical instrumentation and wave damping floats.

Ian Jones, PhD, who is the Director of the Ocean Technology Group at the University of Sydney, has been researching and developing the concept of ocean nourishment for 14 years. His publications include 3 books, over 80 articles, many of them addressing the introduction of nitrogen to the surface ocean and its potential effects on the global carbon cycle and other ocean processes. He is inventor on 7 patents or patent applications [AC: including the application of ammonium salts to stimulate ocean productivity].

Daniel Harrison, GradIEA, has worked on various aspects of ocean nitrogen enrichment and authored several engineering technical reports and a peer reviewed paper on the subject, he also has research experience in applying GIS modeling to fisheries management.

Ryan Roberts, PE, has 12 years of experience designing small naval surface combatants, passenger vessels (CFR Sub-Chap T), naval auxiliaries, ferries, deck barges, tank barges, fishing vessels, and research vessels.

Ryuhei Ishikawa, ME, has 25 years of experience as a mechanical and design engineer. He has directed or teamed on engineering projects involving CO_2 from air capture technology (patented), robotic retrieval systems, organic fermentation process producing organic fertilizer, silicon crystal growing, ferrofluidic sealing technology (high vacuum sealing, clean room sealing, patented), and vibration control.

Adam Cherson, JD-MPA, is the chief executive of Greencore Environmental Information and Research Services. He is the author of *Political*

Ecologies: Essays in Environmental Science and Policy, and *Ecocide: Humanity's Environmental Demons.* He is the publisher-editor of *Political Ecology*, a web-based meta-journal covering environmental sustainability, science, technology, and policy topics. He is a member of the Environmental Law Committee of the Association of the Bar of the City of New York and Scientists Without Borders.

Greg Rau, PhD, (scientific advisor) is a senior researcher with the Institute of Marine Sciences, University of California, Santa Cruz, and also is affiliated with the Carbon Management Program at Lawrence Livermore National Laboratory in Livermore, Calif. His 25-year research career has focused on carbon cycling and biogeochemistry at cellular to global scales, including the development and evaluation CO2 mitigation technologies.

Current Status of Venture

An initial scoping study of the AquaSeq Technology has been performed and points to the technical, economic, and social viability of the goal. A Limited Liability Company has been formed by several members of the development team and a utility patent is pending. A funding proposal seeking US$300,000 has been submitted to the National Science Foundation's Environmental Sustainability Program. The venture is now seeking investment capital to pursue the further development and deployment of a demonstration scale project as well as collaborative research and development partners.

Contact

For further information please contact
Adam Cherson at ac@xyvy.info.

APPENDIX TO EXECUTIVE SUMMARY

Five Year Business Plan Summary

Early Stage Development (Phase 1)

Sub-Phase 1(A): Construction of Pilot Plant Facility (15% of Full Scale capacity)

Business Organization: Limited Liability Company

Part 1: Project Technical Feasibility/Specifications and Parameters/Energy Optimization /Proof and Pilot Plant Funding

Funding Requirement: $500,000.00

Funding Type: Federal Grants and Cooperative Research, LLC Class C Investment (see below for LLC summary)

Terms: Investors become Class C members of AquaSeq, LLC (see below for LLC summary)

Milestone Objective: A) Production of Specification Reports and Proof of Concept and B) Pilot Plant Funding

Completion: A) 6 months from date of funding, B) 12 months from date of funding

Total Time Elapsed to Completion Since Inception: 12 months

<u>**Part 2:** Detailed Design/Engineering and Construction of Pilot Plant Facility</u>

Funding Requirement: $3,500,000.00

Funding Type: LLC Class B or Class C Investment (see below for LLC investment summary)

Terms: Investors become Class B or Class C members of AquaSeq, LLC (see below for LLC summary)

Milestone Objective: Completion of Pilot Plant Facility

Completion: 24 months from funding

Total Time Elapsed to Completion Since Inception: 18 months

<u>**Part 3:** Operation of Pilot Plant Facility/Marketing of System</u>

Milestone Objective: Development Contracts / Funding Commitments for First Full Scale Facility

Completion: 6 months from completion of Pilot Plant

Total Time Elapsed to Completion Since Inception: 30 months

Funding Requirement: None

Sub-Phase 1(B): Development and Operation of First Full Scale Facility

Business Organization: C Corporation

Part 1: Design/Engineering and Construction of First Project Facility

Milestone Objective: Completion of Full Scale Processing Facility

Completion: 12 months from funding

Total Time Elapsed to Completion Since Inception: 42 months

Funding Requirement: $35,000,000.00

Funding Type: Long Term Development Financing, Bond Float, Capital Markets

Terms: Low interest, corporate shares

Part 2: Operation of First Project Facility

Milestone Objective: Revenue production, net profit, begin payback of financing obligations, distributions to shareholders

Completion: Indeterminate

Funding: None

Expansion Stage Development (Phase 2)

Business Organization: Limited Liability Company (see below for LLC structure)

Sub-Phase 2(A): Intensive Marketing of Technology

Milestone Objective: Turnkey Licensing of AquaSeq Technology to Individual developers

Completion: Ongoing

Funding Requirement: Pre-IPO, IPO

Sub-Phase 2(B): Operation as AquaSeq Turnkey Licensor

Milestone Objective: Positive growth rate

Completion: Ongoing

Funding Requirement: None

LLC STRUCTURE SUMMARY

Three Membership Classes: Class A) Managing Members, Class B) Advisory Members, Class C) Convertible Members. New investors may choose between Class B or Class C membership. The same individual may hold memberships in various classes. All classes have distribution rights proportional to capital contribution. Classes A and B have voting powers proportional to capital contributions within their class. Class A holds 70% of the voting power and Class B, 30%. Class C members do not vote but have the yearly option of electing between becoming fully fledged Class B members or withdrawing their capital contribution plus interest pegged to the 1 year United States Treasury Bills on the date of their contribution.

COVER LETTER TO VIRGIN EARTH CHALLENGE[2]

Panel of Judges

Virgin Earth Challenge
Virgin Enterprises Limited
120 Campden Hill Road
London W8 7AR

CONFIDENTIAL

Dear Sirs and Mesdames:

Please accept this entry of the AquaSeq Technology for environmental capture and sequestration for consideration in the Virgin Earth Challenge. Enclosed will be found the challenge checklist, a concept description paper, and a summarizing power point presentation. The AquaSeq Technology may be categorized as a flexible bio-energy with carbon capture and sequestration system.

There is now in place a development team of experienced engineers and scientists ready to discuss any aspect of the AquaSeq Technology in more detail as well as to move into production activities as soon as funding becomes available. I would be glad to provide more information on the development team upon request. Since this is a proprietary, patent pending technology, the panel's confidentiality is appreciated.

In this correspondence I wish to address specifically each of the Assessment Criteria set forth in the Virgin Earth Challenge Terms and Conditions Section 3.

a) Ability of the design to achieve a net removal of a quantifiable amount of GHGs from the atmosphere;

The AquaSeq Technology is designed remove quantifiable and verifiable amounts of environmental Carbon Dioxide. The physical location of the Carbon Dioxide being removed is at the sea surface-atmosphere interface, where it is taken up by photosynthesizing algae. The removal of Carbon Dioxide from this zone means that the surface ocean will be driven to absorb an equal amount of replacement Carbon Dioxide from the atmosphere due to Henry's Law. In an optional configuration of the technology, a portion of the Carbon Dioxide being fed into the AquaSeq system is embodied in other waste biomass materials being used to supplement the algal biomass. In these cases an additional amount of Methane emissions from land fill waste are avoided.

Once inside the system, the Carbon is transformed into a species of inorganic Carbon and then dispersed into the ocean at a minimum depth of 100 meters. The amount of Carbon removed by the system is easily quantifiable by simply taking the weight of the inorganic Carbon that is dispersed into the ocean. The amount of Methane avoidance is easily quantifiable using the Clean Development Mechanism's methodologies. Substantially all of the Carbon being sequestered achieves a net removal due to the system being powered by bio-energy. A comparatively small of amount of Carbon will be released initially in the manufacturing and construction of the processing station (estimated to be about 1.5% for a ten year service life), said amount being overwhelmingly outweighed by the year after year service of the system. Furthermore, the decommissioning costs for the system are essentially zero since the system may be used indefinitely for various non-sequestration purposes after its useful life as a CCS machine.

b) All atmospheric GHGs (not only carbon dioxide) should be considered, in relation to their global warming potential

The AquaSeq Technology is mainly designed to remove atmospheric Carbon Dioxide. Carbon Dioxide is the preponderant anthropogenic greenhouse gas and therefore concentrating on this gas is a wise strategy for environmental capture. Depending on the optional waste biomass configuration chosen, the system is also capable of preventing the release of a substantial amount of Methane as well due to land fill avoidance. Methane is an even more potent atmospheric GHG than Carbon Dioxide although present in much smaller quantities.

The system will also prevent the release of additional quantities of NOx, another potent GHG, by scrubbing and reusing Nitrogen from this gas in the course of the processing sequence.

c) The proposed system should be scalable to a significant size in order to meet the informal removal target of 1 billion tonnes of carbon equivalent per year for 10 years (the "Removal Target") and

d) Ability of the design to achieve the Removal Target. Removal will be considered on a net life cycle basis (i.e., direct and indirect GHG emissions caused by the manufacture, operation and decommissioning of the system should be taken into account);

Each AquaSeq Technology Processing Station is designed to achieve a net removal of 53,209 tonnes of Carbon per year. The total volume removed is entirely dependant on the number of processing stations placed into service. In order to remove 1 billion tonnes per year, about 18,794 processing stations would be needed. The AquaSeq Technology is designed to be sited off-shore, in coastal waters (defined as within the EEZ area). Each station requires an area of about 29 km^2 (less, if waste biomass is used to supplement the algae feedstock). Therefore, the 18,794 processing stations would require the use of 0.56% of the world's EEZ areas or 4.84% of the United States's EEZ.

The AquaSeq Technology is capable of achieving these removal goals on a net life cycle basis. The net operational removal is assured by the system's reliance on internally produced renewable energy, locally available materials, and inexpensive storage infrastructure and monitoring needs. The decommissioning emission costs are drastically reduced if not altogether eliminated by the flexibility of a system that may be put to use even after its life as a CCS machine. Viewed as floating infrastructure, the system may be moved to any coastal area and then deployed as a waste disposal system, or a desalination system, or a renewable energy system, or a fertilizer production plant, or a building materials factory, or any combination of these uses. The system will create emissions in the course of its manufacture which are estimated to be in the 1.5% range for a ten year life cycle and are already calculated into the figures presented in the first paragraph of this section (this rough estimate is based on the construction costs for a 505MW natural gas power plant). The intentional incorporation into this design of existing technologies and off-the-shelf components will help to keep the embodied emissions low and in some cases may even allow the installation of pre-owned equipment and machinery.

e) The system should provide long term GHG removal from the atmosphere. Systems which include potential for GHG release at any point in the cycle will be approached with caution; and

f) The design must show technical viability, effectiveness and efficiency; and

g) Any harmful effects and/or other incidental consequences of the solution should be stated. The proposed system at scale should not create other significant direct or indirect environmental or social damage that would be likely to negate the climate benefit (e.g. extensive ecosystem degradation or significant security threats);

The sequestration mechanism consists of the physical dispersion of inorganic Carbon into the ocean at a depth of 50-100 meters. The efficacy of this system has been evaluated by our team of oceanographers and engineers, as well as other independent researchers, and is considered to be both a durable and ecologically safe means of Carbon storage. Inorganic Carbon is a natural and prevalent component of ocean water. Upon deposition, the receiving layers of water will begin to exchange into deeper waters in the course of a 1000 year cycle of ocean circulation and mixing, meaning that the inorganic Carbon will remain effectively and safely stored for 1000 years or more with little or no need for monitoring. In the interests of scientific accuracy, it must be added that upon fully mixing into the ocean, sometime after 1000 years, when the concentration of inorganic Carbon in surface waters begins to be affected by the earlier deposition, this condition may lead to the off-gassing of Carbon

Dioxide back into the atmosphere. However, if this off-gassing were to occur at all, it would be at a far slower rate than the rate of direct anthropogenic emissions and could be easily dealt with then by a much smaller sequestration and storage system.

The technical viability of the system consists of the fact that the various steps of the process are well known and tested in their various fields of endeavor. A brief list of the mature technologies combined into the AquaSeq Technology includes: Off Shore Processing Platforms, Plasma Pyrolysis, Biomass Gasification, Syngas Polishing and Separation, Water Gas Shift Reaction, Haber (Ammonia) Process, Reverse Osmosis Sea Water Desalination, Modified Solvay (Bicarbonate) Process, Combined Cycle Gas Turbine, Gas to Liquids Conversion (Fischer-Tropsch), Gas Scrubbing, Aquatic Plant Harvesting Vessels, and Trawler Type Fishing Vessels. An offshore system capable of producing and processing 3,000 tonnes per day of biomass and then, by means of these technologies, converting that biomass into energy and inorganic Carbon is technically viable. In spite of its present day technical viability, there are many areas were technological innovation could enhance or improve the efficiency of the process.

Efficiency has many components, each of which needs to be viewed in the context of the others. Clearly one of the most meaningful metrics is the Carbon storage efficiency, or the rate at which the

Carbon taken in by the system is effectively stored. This figure is calculated at 12.15% for the AquaSeq Technology. The system is also expected to consume 222 GJ per tonne of Carbon stored (60.57 GJ per tonne of Carbon Dioxide stored). In order to meaningfully compare these numbers with the efficiencies of other systems it should be remembered that the AquaSeq system is generating its own energy and performing every aspect of the capture and sequestration process, including the capture, the consolidation, the separation, the transformation, the storage, and the monitoring. Secondly, the amount of net Carbon storage is close to 100% due to the fact that life cycle emissions are very low, as discussed in a prior section of this letter. Finally there is the cost efficiency, which varies according to the service life of the technology. A ten year service life yields a cost of $685.97 per tonne (all figures in this paragraph are cost per tonne of net Carbon), a 20 year period, $361.78, and a 30 year period, $253.72. NOTE: This is a cost calculation, not a net cost or net profit calculation, which is presented in the checklist.

The amount of bicarbonate dispersed to the ocean in the course of achieving the Removal Target amounts to .00528 mg per liter of ocean per year. Over 10 years this amounts to .0528 mg per liter of ocean. The current bicarbonate concentration in the oceans is approximately 142 mg/liter. Once the AquaSeq dispersed bicarbonate is fully mixed into the sea it will raise the total ocean concentration to, at most, 142.0528 mg/liter. This is certainly not a harmful concentration considering that salt water aquaria frequently operate at a concentration of 180 to 200 mg/liter (synthetic seawater). A site specific dispersion protocol designed by a team of chemical and physical oceanographers will minimize the risk of excessive localized super-saturation.

One favorable incidental benefit that merits attention is the system's impact on the ocean's acid-base balance. The dispersion of this form of inorganic Carbon to seawater will add alkalinity and thereby help address the other major consequence of rising environmental Carbon Dioxide levels, the acidification of the oceans.

A number of other lesser effects and consequences are discussed in the attached design document. Under appropriate controls and management, these other effects and consequences are not reasonably expected to have substantial negative social or ecological impacts.

h) The system for removal of GHGs must be commercially viable. To this end a clear case should be made for expected return on investment over three and ten years (or longer), taking into account credible scenarios for the future cost of energy, raw materials and management, and future revenue from carbon markets and/or other sources;

Based on various credible scenarios, the commercial viability of the system is summarized in the following four tables.

ITEM	10 YEAR	12 YEAR	20 YEAR	30 YEAR
COSTS				
Operating Cost	$20,000,000	$24,000,000	$40,000,000	$60,000,000
Capital Cost	$345,000,000	$345,000,000	$345,000,000	$345,000,000
Total Cost	$365,000,000	$369,000,000	$385,000,000	$405,000,000
Cost/Tonne(C-seq)	$685.97	$574.78	$361.78	$253.72
REVENUES				
Total Revenue	$328,918,592	$394,702,310	$657,837,184	$986,755,777
Water/Tonne(C-seq)	$155.75	$155.75	$155.75	$155.75
BldMt/Tonne(C-seq)	$67.29	$67.29	$67.29	$67.29
TpFee/Tonne(C-seq)	$395.12	$395.12	$395.12	$395.12
Rev./Tonne(C-seq)	$618.15	$618.15	$618.15	$618.15
NetProfit/Tonne(C-seq)	($67.82)	$40.24	$256.37	$364.43

Table A: Net Profit in Terms of Net Life Cycle Carbon Sequestered (no Carbon Credit Revenues); Notes: revenues from fresh water (@$1.00/m^{3}), building materials (@$15/tonne), and waste tipping fees (33.33% of biomass input from waste @$60/tonne).

ITEM	10 YEAR	11 YEAR	20 YEAR	30 YEAR
COSTS				
Operating Cost	$20,000,000	$22,000,000	$40,000,000	$60,000,000
Capital Cost	$345,000,000	$345,000,000	$345,000,000	$345,000,000
Total Cost	$365,000,000	$367,000,000	$385,000,000	$405,000,000
Cost/Tonne(C-seq)	$685.97	$627.03	$361.78	$253.72
REVENUES				
Total Revenue	$355,928,592	$391,521,451	$711,857,184	$1,067,785,777
Water/Tonne(C-seq)	$155.75	$155.75	$155.75	$155.75
BldMt/Tonne(C-seq)	$67.29	$67.29	$67.29	$67.29
TpFee/Tonne(C-seq)	$395.12	$395.12	$395.12	$395.12
Credit/Tonne(C-seq)	$50	$50	$50	$50
Rev./Tonne(C-seq)	$668.15	$668.15	$668.15	$668.15
NetProfit/Tonne(C-seq)	($17.05)	$41.90	$307.14	$415.20

Table B: Net Profit in Terms of Net Life Cycle Carbon Sequestered (with Carbon Credit Revenues); Notes: revenues from fresh water (@$1.00/m$^{3)}$, building materials (@$15/tonne), waste tipping fees (33.33% of biomass input from waste @$60/tonne), carbon credits (@$50/tonne)

YEARS	NO CARB CREDITS	YES CARB CREDITS
10	($678,241,773,008)	($170,484,095,296)
11	($97,679,399,162)	$460,845,516,475
12	$482,882,974,685	$1,092,175,128,246
20	$5,127,381,965,457	$6,142,812,022,414
30	$10,933,005,703,922	$12,456,108,140,124

Table C: Total Net Profit: Sequestration of 1 Billion Tonnes-C(eq)/Year

YEARS	NO CARB CREDITS	YES CARB CREDITS
10	-1.05%	-0.26%
11	-0.14%	0.65%
12	0.62%	1.40%
20	3.95%	4.74%
30	5.62%	6.40%

Table D: Annualized Return on Equity

These four tables reveal that under a fixed cost and fixed revenue scenario, using midrange pricing values, the Target Removal of 1 Billion Tonnes per year does not break even until the 11th or 12th years (depending on inclusion of revenue from credits). However, once the break even point is reached, net profits begin to accumulate quickly so that by the 20th or 30th years, total profits have risen to US$10.9 Trillion or US$12.4 Trillion. This rapidly accelerating profit picture is due to the fact that the system is substantially self-sufficient as to materials and energy. On a thirty year time frame return on equity between 5.62% and 6.40% per annum (subject to plant maintenance and replacement costs that will increase with an aging stock). What these numbers suggest is that the commercial viability of the AquaSeq Technology is dependant on taking an 11-30 year horizon, and that even from a 30 year perspective the returns on equity are on the order of a 30 year fixed rate mortgage or industrial bond (as of this writing 30 year fixed rate mortgage rates are at 5.14% and the

Moody's yield index on seasoned 'Aaa' industrial bonds is at 5.26%).

Since it appears from present emissions projections that ten years of 1 Billion Tonne per year removal may not be a sufficient amount of Carbon removal from the perspective of ecological health, then, for both commercial and ecological reasons, the business model for the carbon capture and sequestration industry should adopt a 30 year time horizon, or longer. This is also a reasonable service life and depreciation period for a capital asset of this type.

Commercial viability is not only a product of the profits and rates of return. It is also important to evaluate the relative strength of the business model from other intangible perspectives such as: 1) the differentiation of the technology from other ACCS strategies, 2) the valuation added by the technology, and 3) the people proposition of the system (ways in which the technology interacts with socio-political factors).

Differentiation: Unlike many other ACCS strategies, AquaSeq offers a range of operational configuration options, from a fully self contained, 'under one roof' strategy to a variable feedstock input strategy. Depending on market, environmental, and other conditions surrounding any particular installation, the optimal operational configuration may be selected from a wide range of options to assure commercial viability.

The 'under one roof strategy' consists of biomass harvesting, energy production, chemical transformation, and sea water dispersion all within a compact geographical area, eliminating the need for complicated concentration, piping, and transportation infrastructures to move the Carbon from collection points to industrial facilities to potentially far flung sequestration points.

The variable feedstock strategy involves receiving and processing, subject to equipment adjustments, practically any carbon containing feedstock including crop residues, carbon crops, other agricultural wastes, municipal solid waste, sewage sludge, marine debris, refuse derived fuel, mineralized carbon from other types of carbon capture technologies, and plastics.

Finally, the Carbon storage strategy offered by AquaSeq is unlike many others in that it consists of the simple dispersion of solid inorganic Carbon into the mid-epipelagic zone (50-100 meters). Due to the chemical and physical properties of the ocean system, this sequestration strategy drastically reduces storage and monitoring costs.

Valuation added: The flexibility of uses during the sequestration service greatly enhances the return on equity of the installation as demonstrated in Tables A-D. However, there is another form of flexibility that adds values to this infrastructure: AquaSeq may be moved and adapted, post-sequestration, for solid waste (including agricultural waste, sewage solids, and marine debris) disposal, landfill reclamation, hazardous waste disposal, waste-to-energy conversion, water desalination, renewable energy (producing any combination of electricity, liquid fuels, and/or Hydrogen), fertilizer production, animal feeds production, Lithium production, Uranium production, building and road construction materials manufacture, or any combination thereof. The system may be adapted to produce any one or more of the following products: Syngas, Hydrogen, liquid fuels, electricity, heat, Argon, Methane, Lithium, Deuterium, Uranium, Ammonium Chloride, and vitreous slag for use as a building material or hydroponic soil medium. This post-sequestration utility is not incorporated into Tables A-D since they are only a thirty year projection.

People proposition: There are several ways the AquaSeq process addresses social, political, and people issues associated with greenhouse gas mitigation strategies. First, the use of offshore locations minimizes land use and coastal esthetics conflicts. Second, the use of established technologies and off-the-shelf equipment opens up a range of strategic partnerships, vendor and supply chain relationships, and skilled labor opportunities that are sure to appeal to many existing industries and labor unions. For instance, existing energy or petrochemical companies, their suppliers, and their laborers can easily make a lateral move to this technology. Third, the ability of this system to be installed locally (within the EEZ of developed nations) but with global impact may help to overcome the political logjam between developed and developing nations regarding the burdens and costs of remediation for prior emissions. Fourth, this system would create a new type of infrastructure for developing nations to meet their growing fresh water, fertilizer, waste disposal, and renewable energy needs. Fifth, sea water dispersion of inorganic Carbon is more likely to meet with approval from environmentalists and other stakeholders than enhanced oil recovery or geological/seabed burial. Sixth, the synthesis of 'green' technologies brought together by this system will function as a development cluster, spawning new methods and technologies of economic value.

i) The proposed mechanism for measurement of carbon removed should be sufficiently credible (1) to accurately monitor the system's performance over time; and (2) to enable revenue generation on the regulatory and/or voluntary carbon market (if applicable to the commercial viability);

The sequestration strategy utilized in the AquaSeq Technology is straightforward and measurable, suggesting a more direct route to CDM approval for carbon credit financing than some of the other options on the market (i.e., additionality, permanence, fugacity, and leakage concerns are minimized). The accuracy of monitoring is achieved in several ways: first, the amount of Carbon being stored is a direct measurement of the tonnage of inorganic Carbon being dispersed. Second, the effect of the dispersion can be measured over time by means of the various global ocean sensing systems already in place. These systems will sense significant changes in total inorganic Carbon, alkalinity, pH, and with respect to Carbon Dioxide, the sea level atmospheric partial pressure and surface water concentrations. The resulting combination of these measurements will provide evidence that the fate of the dispersed Carbon. Third, our scientific team is exploring the possibility of chemically identifying or tracing the Carbon stored by the system so that its fate can be more accurately be studied over time. The combination of these monitoring strategies will support the designation of this technology as an approved CDM methodology as well as the fungibility of AquaSeq credits on all the Carbon trading exchanges. Nevertheless, the commercial viability of the technology is not dependent on Carbon credit revenues due to the uncertainty over the market pricing for such credits.

j) If applicable, any other contributions to the reduction in environmental GHGs should be stated;

The AquaSeq Technology makes a number of ancillary contributions to greenhouse gas reduction, some of which have already been mentioned. First, there is the creation of simultaneous byproducts using carbon neutral energy. Second, there is the potential use of many types of waste as feedstocks, thereby avoiding the creation of methane from waste decomposition. Third, the entire system can be converted to a renewable energy or biofuels plant following the period of sequestration use, thus becoming a player in the post-fossil fuel economy. Substantial amounts of electricity, heat, and/or liquid fuels can be produced from a variety of feedstocks. Fourth, the plant can be converted into a renewable energy fueled producer of fresh water, fertilizer, building materials, and other specialty chemicals.

k) The proposed operation for each entry must be demonstrable at least in the laboratory environment prior to final judging;

The AquaSeq Technology may be demonstrated in miniature under laboratory conditions. A team of scientists and engineers is assembled and ready to perform this task prior to the final judging, given sufficient time to arrange for the demonstration.

l) There should be clarity as to ownership of intellectual property in the design submission. This is likely to be assessed at later stages of the selection process, but any concerns should be identified.

The AquaSeq technology owned by Adam Cherson and is pending a patent before the United States Patent and Trademark Office.

In the interests of global environmental health and human well being, I encourage the panel to delve as deeply as necessary into the system described in these papers, including as much discussion as desired with the specialized engineers and scientists familiar with the project.

Very Truly Yours,

Adam Cherson

SUSTAINABLE GLOBAL CHANGE INFRASTRUCTURE

Innocentive Challenge ID: 9673018

The Challenge

In February 2011, The Economist will be hosting a conference to discuss the topic of Intelligent Infrastructure as a part of their Ideas Economy conference series. As with The Economist's September 2010 Conference on Human Potential, Innocentive and The Economist are teaming up to run a Challenge as a means of recognizing and drawing attention to promising ideas that address one of the conference's themes – global climate change. This ideation Challenge, sponsored by the Economist and Innocentive, seeks to engage our innovative and talented communities and channel your insights into the conference. Ultimately the winning Solver of this Challenge will be asked to participate and possibly speak or be interviewed at the conference. The specifics of the Challenge are outlined below.

The need to reduce atmospheric carbon is of tremendous global importance since it is widely understood to be the primary driver of climate change. As part of those efforts, numerous approaches of reducing atmospheric carbon are currently under exploration. These ideas range from mere evolutionary innovations to revolutionary geo-engineering projects, and many have garnered significant research attention and financial support.

Some of the most interesting and potentially viable projects currently being explored fall into the realm of geo-engineering. For example within geo-engineering, in the domain of synthetic biology, scientists are exploring new means of efficiently fixing carbon by engineering carbon-consuming microbes that could be introduced into the environment. The theory is that such microbes could be deployed and activated selectively to fix carbon on demand, in an inducible and tunable manner. Those developments are currently being explored within a highly controlled laboratory setting but ultimately a successful solution will need to be both scalable and economical in order to be truly viable.

This Challenge seeks to identify promising ideas for BIOLOGICAL capture and sequestration of atmospheric carbon dioxide. A valued submission will suggest a solution that can scale up over time and be economically viable, and it will include any preliminary evidence that supports claims of the viability and functionality of the Solver's idea.

The Solution

REFERENCE TITLE OF THE INVENTION-CONCEPT

Sustainable Global Change Infrastructure (SGC-I): System and Methods for the Capture, Sequestration, and Storage of Carbon

Statement Regarding FUNDING

The Solver has invested approximately $3,000.00 out-of-pocket towards the development of this invention-concept.

PRELIMINARY EVIDENCE AND REFERENCES

The attached document, "Supporting Research and Evidence," contains a list of journal references and other sources used by the Solver to assess the technical and economic viability of the invention-concept.

Abstract of the INVENTION

The core of the SGC-I consists of an apparatus used for sequestering carbon wherein the said apparatus dissociates a carbon containing feedstock material and reacts the resulting gases with a system-produced brine to create four products: 1) a sodium based carbonate or bicarbonate, 2) ammonium chloride, 3) fresh water, and 4) a multi-purpose building material. End product (1) may be sequestered in any of several ways for durable and long term storage. End product (2) may be used for oceanic nutrient enrichment or other economically valuable purposes. End products (3) and (4) may be distributed to human populations.

The SGC-I further consists of a complete system and method for capturing or removing carbon dioxide from the environment prior to the sequestering and also for the storing away of the carbon for a geologically significant period of time after the sequestering. The system consists of four major steps, or segments: capture, sequestration (split into separation and transformation), and storage. There are numerous possible embodiments for each of these steps. The preferred embodiment along with several major alternate embodiments are described in the detailed description. In each of the embodiments a carbon-containing feedstock is processed into a storage product and several co-products. A schematic overview of such a system is shown in the block diagram of *Figure 1*, in accordance with the preferred embodiment of the invention. The processing station may be located on land or at sea and the feedstock may be any carbon-containing material. The preferred embodiment comprises an offshore algae farm and adjoining offshore processing station. The algae farm surrounds the processing plant and produces a flow of carbon-containing feedstock for the station. The feedstock is cultivated and harvested and then brought to the processing station where it is thermally separated to form a product gas. A series of chemical transformations of this product gas leads to various intermediary and end products which are then re-used in the process (N_2, CO, CO_2, H_2, NaCl, Syngas, and H_2O), are dispersed and sequestered back into the environment ($NaHCO_3$, NH_4Cl, vitreous slag), and are transported away from the system for use in human civilization (H2O, NH_4Cl, building materials). In an alternate embodiment, the SGC-I may produce and process micro-algae, whether of natural origin or as genetically enhanced. In another embodiment, feedstock materials that have been produced or captured elsewhere and are imported into the system may also be processed. In an alternate embodiment, the SGC-I may be producing its own feedstock and importing feedstocks, simultaneously.

BRIEF DESCRIPTION OF THE SEVERAL VIEWS OF THE DRAWING

Figure 1: presents a black box diagram representing an overview of the SGC-I showing the inputs and outputs of the preferred embodiment.

Figure 2: presents a black box diagram representing an overview of the SGC-I showing the inputs and outputs of an alternate embodiment.

Figure 3: presents a detailed block diagram representing the major steps and sub-steps of the process in the preferred embodiment.

Figure 4: presents an exemplary illustration showing the offshore macro-algae farm layout of the preferred embodiment.

Figure 5: presents an exemplary illustration showing the harvest and dispersion vessel in the preferred embodiment.

Figure 6: presents an exemplary illustration showing the macro-algae enclosure system in the preferred embodiment.

Figure 7: (A:left, B:center, C:right) presents an exemplary illustration showing the processing station in a preferred embodiment for vessel dispersion of end products.

Figure 8: (A:left, B:center, C:right) presents an exemplary illustration showing the processing station in a preferred embodiment for direct dispersion of end products.

BACKGROUND OF THE INVENTION

It is well known in the science and policy of global greenhouse gas mitigation that aversion of potentially harmful environmental carbon levels requires three paths of action: (a) the reduction of newly created carbon; (b) the capture, sequestration, and storage of newly created carbon at a point of emission; and (c) the capture, sequestration, and storage of previously released carbon already in the environment. This invention pertains to either the second and third of these paths of action by providing a system to capture, sequester, transform, and store newly or previously released carbon.

Many carbon capture, sequestration, and storage (CCSS) concepts have been proposed and discussed in the scientific literature. The essential characteristics of these various concepts is summarized in Table 1. The most prevalent of these involve the capture of CO_2 directly from flue gas or via coal gasification, often combined with enhanced oil recovery or bioenergy production. Other options for storage of flue gas captured CO_2 include geological, mineral, or ocean storage. A second type of proposal involves processes for the direct chemical capture of CO_2 from the atmosphere followed by any of the above storage strategies. A final strategy seeks to stimulate natural processes and cycles to accelerate CCSS. This category includes reforestation, aforestation, prevention of deforestation, enhanced carbonate formation, and oceanic nourishment or fertilization. These strategies enlist living biomass, seawater, or soil (including biochar) storage strategies. Related to all three major strategies are efforts to improve chemical or biological capture efficiencies via new methods and materials, and to find secure and ample geological storage reservoirs.

While the prior literature offers numerous technologies for CCSS, it is respectfully submitted that none of those thus far offered provides an immediately executable and sustainable strategy for reducing greenhouse gases on the scale of 1 billion metric tons of carbon equivalents per year. These are the levels of sequestration that will be needed if CCSS is to have any impact on global geochemistry and climate (Pacala, S and Socolow, R. 2004. Stabilization Wedges: Solving the Climate Problem for the Next 50 Years with Current Technologies. Science, 305(5686), pp 968-972. New York, NY. doi: 10.1126/science.1100103). The above systems pose varying obstacles to their implementation at a large scale: 1) land use demands and conflicts, 2) net process energy losses and life cycle carbon positivity, 3) geographic fragmentation of capture mechanisms and a corresponding need for massive pipeline and/or transportation system to collect, concentrate, and sequester CO_2, 4) availability of and access to process input materials, 5) availability and/or efficacy of geological formations suitable for storage, 6) impermanence of storage, 7) complexity of infrastructure and retrofitting demands, 8) creation of chemical wastes, 9) lack of economic co-benefits, and 10) lack of co-uses as beneficial infrastructure beyond the CCSS applications.

The SGC-I described here is substantially novel and unlike any prior art due not only to its chemical engineering design, but also in that it creates a fully integrated and self-contained method of CCSS able to overcome the challenges to immediacy, effectiveness and sustainability mentioned in the prior paragraph. The result is a system that minimizes negative environmental impacts; minimizes interference with existing or potential human activities; minimizes infrastructure fragmentation and complexity; requires easily obtainable and plentiful natural resources; is substantially energy self-reliant; sequesters sufficient quantities of carbon, quickly enough, to have a meaningful impact on environmental levels; creates byproducts of economic value to help defray economic costs; and is adaptable to other production or industrial uses such as renewable energy, fresh water, plant fertilizers, animal feeds, industrial chemicals, solid waste processing, and waste to energy creation. The present SGC-I's essential characteristic resides in its innovative combination of treatment steps, integrating and unifying the capture, sequestration, and storage aspects of CCSS so as to improve substantially upon the prior literature.

DETAILED DESCRIPTION OF THE INVENTION

In accordance with the preferred embodiment of the SGC-I, the system comprises a processing platform placed so as to be in relatively close proximity to both the source of input materials going into the system, and the final destination of the processed products produced by the system. The input materials required by the process are a carbon-containing feedstock, saltwater, ambient air, and in certain alternate embodiments, natural sand. The processed products are sodium bicarbonate, ammonium chloride, fresh water, building materials, and, in certain alternate embodiments, a sodium-carbonate-slag storage material. The processing platform should be equally distant from the point where the carbon capture will occur, the point where the carbon storage will occur, and the point where the useful co-products will be delivered. In the preferred embodiment, the carbon capture step comprises the cultivation of marine macro-algae and occurs in an area adjacent to the processing plant. In the preferred embodiment, the carbon storage occurs in the unmixed layers of the ocean which begins generally 200 meters below the surface of the ocean and at the edge of the continental shelf. In the preferred embodiment, the useful co-products are be delivered to the closest shipping port. In the preferred embodiment the placement of the processing platform is in an offshore, coastal zone, where saltwater and sand are readily available, where an algae growing area is readily available, and where the processed products may be dispersed or delivered with the least amount of effort to their respective destinations. In embodiments where the carbon-containing feedstock is imported into the system, proximity to the source of this feedstock should also be considered.

The description of this preferred embodiment is not intended to be limiting in any form or manner. Other carbon inputs may be considered as separate embodiments, used as available to replace or complement the algae crop. Examples of other carbon inputs include, but are not limited to: other crops including land-based crops or micro-algae, municipal residue biomass, agricultural wastes, sewage sludge, timber milling wastes, refuse derived fuel, paper making wastes, ethanol and other biofuel-making wastes, construction wastes, carbon captured from the environment or from industrial flue gases using alternative biological, chemical, or mechanical means. In each of these cases, the carbon containing material is brought to the processing station and is subjected to the remaining process steps alone or in combination with any other carbon feedstocks.

Capture Step: While any photosynthesizing plant or algae or combination thereof may be considered as a separate embodiment, free-floating marine macro-algae, of one or more species, grown in offshore enclosures are presented here as the preferred embodiment. *Reference is made to Figure 4* which schematically illustrates an exemplary growing-processing area included in the system, in accordance with the preferred embodiment of the invention. The growing-processing area described is not intended to be limiting in any form or manner, and it should be evident to a person skilled in the art that the growing-processing area may be implemented in other ways. Furthermore, the growing-processing area described is ocean-based, although in other SGC-I embodiments the growing-processing area may be land-based (and may optionally include inland water bodies), or combined land-ocean-based (partially on land and partially on water). In other embodiments, algae of any type and growth habit may be grown in unenclosed, open ocean areas, in other types of ocean enclosures, inland water bodies, combined land-ocean based systems, land-based agricultural fields, or land-based enclosures. Each of these alternative embodiments will require adaptations that will be evident to a person skilled in the art.

Each growing-processing area includes one or more crop circles wherein the algae is grown, surrounded, for example, by a moored, floating skirt to prevent the algal growth from separating and drifting as shown in *Figures 4 and 6*. The growing-processing area further includes a process station which includes one or more separation reactors as well as other process reactors and sub-systems required by the method.

In the preferred SGC-I embodiment, the free-floating macro-algae are cultivated by a combination of natural circulation of currents and by the surface dispersion of ammonium produced by the system. The ammonium is dispersed by the same vessels used to harvest the algae as shown schematically in *Figure 5*. In the preferred embodiment, the algae are harvested on to the vessels by means of an inclined ramp inserted obliquely into the surface growing area. The inclined ramp is equipped with automated cutting blades to prevent entanglement. The harvested material is delivered mechanically up the ramp and into the vessel's algae hold where it is subjected to mechanical compression to both dewater the algae and create additional storage space. The harvest and fertilization vessel described is not intended to be limiting in any form or manner, and it should be evident to a person skilled in the art that the harvesting and fertilization may be implemented in other ways. In land-based systems, for example, the harvest transport vessels may comprise trucks or trains, or other land-based transport means.

Following the harvesting and dewatering, the algae are transported by the same vessels to the processing platform where they may be mixed as necessary with other feedstock materials to arrive at an optimal mass ratio which, for exemplary purposes, may comprise 40% carbon, 35% inorganic elements, and 25% water. The ratio of the various feedstock materials may be adjusted by a person skilled in the art, according to the properties of the algae, by altering the amounts of other inputs such as process captured CO_2, seawater, natural sand, or other carbon-containing materials imported to the system.

Sequestration 1: Separation Step: The next stage of the process comprises the thermal separation or depolymerization of the feedstock. In the preferred embodiment, thermal depolymerization is effected without combustion at high heat temperatures (>900°C) by plasma arch technology. In other embodiments, the thermal separation is effected with combustion at medium heat temperatures (300°C and 900°C) by pyrolysis technology, or by low heat temperatures (<300°C) by gasification technology. In the preferred embodiment the heat energy is provided by a portion of the biomass as fuel. In other embodiments, the heat energy is provided by concentrated solar power or by wind energy. In yet other embodiments, the thermal separation may be effected by a combination of heat temperatures and technologies. The thermal separation technologies may be selected and adjusted for temperature, pressure, catalysts, and thermal media by persons skilled in the art of biomass depolymerization, combustion and catalysis. In the preferred embodiment, thermal depolymerization creates a product gas and a vitreous slag of variable composition.

In the preferred embodiment, this product gas is separated into several derivative gas streams. Some of the product gas is diverted to a water-gas-shift reactor for the production of H_2 to be used in the ammonia production stage as described further on below. N_2 and CO_2 are separated from the product gas using, in the preferred embodiment, permeable membrane technologies and are then diverted for use in the ammonia and bicarbonate stages described below. The remaining product gas is cleaned and polished to create a Syngas for process energy uses either as electricity generated by combined cycle turbines, or as bunker oil for the various transportation needs of the system, produced using Fischer-Tropsch, or other energy technologies. Heat exchange technologies are used throughout to capture and re-use waste heat.

In accordance with an embodiment of the invention, the system is adapted to supply substantial portions of its own energy needs. Additional energy inputs such as wind or solar generation, or biodiesel from outside the system, may be used to compensate for insufficient amounts of net energy derived from the algae.

Sequestration 2: Transformation Step: *Ammonia Production:* In accordance with an embodiment of the invention, ammonia may be produced using the Haber process. The process involves passing reactants several times over a catalyst until a yield of approximately 98% is achieved. The basic formula for this step is:

$$N_2(g) + 3H_2(g) \rightarrow 2NH_3(g), \Delta Ho = -92.4\ kJ/mol$$

Useful byproducts may be recovered from the Haber process. As mentioned earlier, the ammonia synthesis reactants are looped over the catalyst several times, and both argon and methane tend to accumulate in the loop, requiring removal. In some embodiments of the invention, the recovered argon may serve as an inert medium in the separation reactor. Optionally, the recovered methane may be blended into the separation step product gas for transformation into useful energy.

Transformation Step: *Brine Production:* In accordance with the preferred embodiment of the invention, a constant stream of brine (concentrated sea water) is needed for sodium-bicarbonate production. For purposes of this exemplary description, conventional reverse osmosis membrane desalination may be used, although other desalination methods and sub-systems may be used in other embodiments. For example, thermal desalination methods with or without fresh water recovery may be used. Desalination may be powered either by fuels produced within the process or by solar/wind energy generated at the facility. The final briny water solution is supplied to the sodium-bicarbonate sub-step. In some embodiments of the invention, the remaining fresh water is available for human use, for example, both within and outside the system. Optionally, the remaining sea water is available for production (extraction) of Lithium, Uranium, and other rare elements.

In some embodiments of the SGC-I, the desalination sub-step may require an additive to prevent corrosion of components. For example, the additive may include Chlorine as an anti-fouling agent, and which may be obtained from the sodium-bicarbonate step where ammonium chloride is a byproduct. Optionally, the desalination components may be partially, or wholly, constructed from an anti-corrosive materials. Following recovery from the desalination system, the ammonium chloride may be added back to the dispersion stock. In some embodiments of the invention, chlorine may also be added to the freshwater product to prevent fouling.

Transformation Step: *Sodium-Bicarbonate and Ammonium Chloride Production:* In accordance with the preferred embodiment of the invention, a modified version of the Solvay process is adapted to produce sodium-bicarbonate for storage. This end product is reached in one step:

$$NaCl+NH_3+H_2O+CO_2 \rightarrow NaHCO_3+NH_4Cl$$

The ammonium chloride and the sodium bicarbonate are thermo-chemically separated and diverted to their ultimate dispersion systems described in subsequent steps.

In an alternate SGC-I embodiment, a sodium-carbonate-slag material is produced for storage purposes. In this alternative embodiment, the ammonium chloride is separated out thermo-chemically while the sodium bicarbonate is heated according to this reaction:

$$2NaHCO_3 + HEAT \rightarrow Na_2CO_3+H_2O+CO_2$$

The product water resulting from the process may be either added to the desalination fresh water product or discharged. The CO_2 may be partially recycled back into the first step of the sodium-bicarbonate reaction with the remainder optionally sent back to the separation reactor or released to the atmosphere. Furthermore, in this alternate embodiment, silica has been combined with the other feedstocks into the separation step to produce a vitreous slag. The vitreous slag is partially cooled to a temperature high enough so that the slag retains enough elasticity to allow mechanical mixing with the sodium carbonate (Na_2CO_3) yet sufficiently low to prevent the sodium carbonate from disassociating. The resulting sodium-carbonate-slag material is then deposited to the sea bottom or other geological formation for storage. In one such embodiment, Silica (sand) is taken from a surface or sea bottom terrain and the manufactured sodium-carbonate-slag gravel is put in its place. For example, this procedure may comprise a shallow water dredge mining operation. Optionally, the procedure may comprise a deep water dredge mining operation. Optionally, the procedure may comprise a land-based operation. In another embodiment, the sodium-carbonate-slag material is cooled to 1-2 inch pea-gravel size and dispersed directly into the sea either from the processing platform or from a dispersion vessel, whereupon the material will sink to the bottom for permanent storage. In another embodiment, the sodium-carbonate-slag material is cooled into pea-gravel, building bricks, or other useful forms as a building material and shipped to a commercial port.

Storage and Dispersion Steps: According to the preferred embodiment, the sodium bicarbonate product is mechanically injected from the processing platform into the unmixed layer of the ocean (below

200m) through retractable tubing. The bicarbonate is expected to remain sequestered in the unmixed zone for at least 6,000 years. Alternatively, the sodium bicarbonate is taken by ship to another area where it may be injected from the ship into the unmixed layer of the ocean (below 200m) through retractable tubing.

In the preferred embodiment, the ammonium chloride is dispersed by the harvesting vessel to fertilize the algae crop. Furthermore, any ammonium chloride not taken up by the algae will be carried by currents to other areas of the ocean where it will continue to fertilize phytoplankton and thereby increase the biomass of these areas, including possibly the biomass of higher trophic level organisms such as fish, marine mammals, and sea birds. In an alternative embodiment, the ammonium chloride may be shipped off-site for use in animal feeds, plant fertilization, or advanced biofuel production.

Other Uses and Products: In some embodiments of the SGC-I, the method may be adapted to have other productive and industrial purposes that are not related to CCSS. This multitasking flexibility may help to justify capital expenditures required for such a project by providing a useful life beyond CCSS. In one exemplary embodiment, the mobility of the processing platform means that they may be moved to other areas for other uses, similar to floating oil drill rigs today. In one exemplary embodiment, the system may be moved to an area of excessive nutrient loading to collect and process macro-algal blooms, thereby remediating a condition of hazardous eutrophication. In another exemplary embodiment, the system may be moved to an area of marine debris to collect and process the floating trash. In another exemplary embodiment, the system may be used to process carbon that has been captured from existing power generation or industrial facilities (end of pipe capture) and been transported to the system. In other embodiments, possible non-CCSS uses of the system may include, for example, solid waste disposal (including sewage solids and biofuel wastes), landfill reclamation, hazardous waste disposal, water desalination, renewable energy creation (any combination of electricity, heat, liquid fuels, and/or Hydrogen), fertilizer and feeds production, metals production, lithium production, sea-water uranium extraction, building and road construction materials, or other combinations thereof. Due to this flexibility of uses, the system need not be decommissioned when, and if, the CCSS purpose becomes moot.

The preferred embodiment of the system describes a single processing platform. It may be evident to a person skilled in the art that the system may be expanded to include numerous processing platforms so as to capture and sequester additional amounts of carbon. In an alternate embodiment, enough platforms could be deployed to sequester and store, for example, 80% of the annual CO_2 emissions of the United States, or 80% of world's annual CO_2 emissions, or 1 billion metric tons of carbon equivalents or any other amount, or simply to be used for other useful purposes without any consideration of carbon emission levels or atmospheric concentrations.

Sustainable Global Change Infrastructure (SGC-I)

SUPPORTING RESEARCH AND EVIDENCE

Baciocchi, R, et al. Process design and energy requirements for the capture of Carbon Dioxide from air. Chemical Engineering and Processing, 2006, 45(12), pp 1047-1058. doi:10.1016/j.cep.2006.03.015

Banerjee, R, et al. High-Throughput Synthesis of Zeolitic Imidazolate Frameworks and Application to CO_2 Capture. Science 15 February 2008: Vol. 319. no. 5865, pp. 939 – 943. doi: 10.1126/science.1152516

Boyd, PW. Ranking geo-engineering schemes. Nature Geoscience, 2008, 1, pp. 722-724. doi:10.1038/ngeo348

Brown, T, et al. Hydrothermal Liquefaction and Gasification of *Nannochloropsis sp.* Energy and Fuels, 2010, 24 (6), 3639-3646. doi: 10.1021/ef100203u

Butterman, HC and Castaldi, MJ. CO2 as Carbon Neutral Fuel Source via Enhanced Biomass Gasification. Environ. Sci. Technol., 2009, 43(23), pp 930–937. doi. 10.1021/es901509n

Butterman, H.C. and M.J. Castaldi, Influence of CO_2 Injection on Biomass Gasification, Ind. Eng. Chem. Res., Vol.(46), pp. 8875-8886, 2007. doi: 10.1021/ie071160n

Caldeira, K and Rau, G. Accelerating carbonate dissolution to sequester carbon dioxide in the ocean: Geochemical implications. Geophysical Research Letters, 2000, Vol. 27, No. 2, pp.225-228. http://www.agu.org/pubs/crossref/2000/1999GL002364.shtml

California Integrated Waste Management Board. Evaluation of Conversion Technology

Processes and Products, Appendix G: Description of Plasma Arc Processes from Survey Responses. 2004. http://biomass.ucdavis.edu/materials/reports%20and%20publications/2004/2004_Conversion_Technology_Appendices.pdf

Carlsson, AS, et al. Micro- and Macro-Algae: Utility for Industrial Applications. CPL Press, UK, 2007. http://www.epobio.net/news/news070917.htm.

Chynoweth, DP, et al. "Biological Gasification of Marine Algae" in Bird, K. T. and Benson, P. H., eds.

Seaweed Cultivation for Renewable Resources, 285-303, Elsevier, New York, 1987.

http://www.agen.ufl.edu/~chyn/download/Publications_DC/Book%20Chapters/1987%20-%20Biological%20Gasification....pdf

Corradetti, A, et al. Should Biomass be Used for Power Generation or Hydrogen Production? J. Eng. Gas Turbines Power, 2007, 129(3), pp 629-637. http://dx.doi.org/10.1115/1.2718226

Dong, Zhou, et al. Hydrothermal Liquefaction of Macroalgae *Enteromorpha prolifera* to Bio-oil. Energy Fuels, 2010, 24(7), 4054-4061. doi: 10.1021/ef100151h

Elliott, DC and Sealock, Jr., LJ. Chemical Processing in High-Pressure Aqueous Environments: Low Temperature Catalytic Gasification. Trans IchemE, 1996, 74(A).
www.pnl.gov/biobased/docs/chem_processing.pdf

Fridman, A. Plasma Chemistry. Cambridge University Press, 2008.

Fu, Qingxi, et al. Syngas production via high-temperature steam/CO2 co-electrolysis: an economic assessment. Energy and Environmental Science, 2010, (3), 1382-1397. doi: 10.1039/C0EE00092B

Fulke, AB, et al. Bio-mitigation of CO2, calcite formation and simultaneous biodiesel precursors production using *Chlorella* sp. Bioresource Technology, 2010, 101 (21), 8473-8476. doi:10.1016/j.biortech.2010.06.012

Gallagher, BJ. The economics of producing biodiesel from algae. Renewable Energy, 2011 36 (1), 158-162. doi: 10.1016/j.renene.2010.06.016

Gao, K and McKinley, KR. Use of macroalgae for marine biomass production and CO_2 remediation: a review. Journal of Applied Phycology, 1994, 6, pp. 45-60. doi: 10.1007/BF02185904

Hanisak, MD and Samuel, MA. Growth Rates in Culture of Several Species of *Sargassum* from Florida, USA, Hydrobiologia, 1987, 151/152, pp 399-404. http://dx.doi.org/10.1007BF00046159

Haszeldine, RS. Carbon Capture and Storage: How Green Can Black Be? Science, 2009, 325, pp. 1647-1652. doi: 10.1126/science.1172246

Hicks, J, et al. Designing Adsorbents for CO_2 Capture from Flue Gas-Hyperbranched Aminosilicas Capable of Capturing CO_2 Reversibly. J. Am. Chem. Soc., 2008, 130 (10), pp 2902–2903. doi: 10.1021/ja077795v

Huczko, A. Plasma decomposition of Carbon Dioxide. AIChE Journal, 2004, 30(5), pp 811-815. http://dx.doi.org/10.1002/aic.690300517

Intergovenmental Panel on Climate Change, Fourth Assessment Report, 2007, http://www.ipcc.ch/pdf/assessment-report/ar4/syr/ar4_syr.pdf

Jones, ISF & Caldeira, K. Long-term ocean carbon sequestration with macronutrient addition. Engineering Carbon Sequestration in the Ocean, Second Annual Conference on Carbon Sequestration, May 2003. http://www.netl.doe.gov/publications/proceedings/03/carbon-seq/PDFs/110.pdf

Jones, ISF & Lu, CH. Engineering Carbon Sequestration in the Ocean, Second Annual Conference on Carbon Sequestration, May 2003. http://ses.library.usyd.edu.au/handle/2123/986

Jones, ISF, and Young, HE. The Potential of the Ocean for the Management of Global Warming. Int. J. of Global Warming, 2009, 1(1/2/3) pp. 43-56. doi: 10.1504/IJGW.2009.027080

Judd, B; Harrison, DP; Jones, ISF. Engineering Ocean Nourishment. Proceedings of the World Congress on Engineering, 2008, Vol II, WCE 2008

(ISBN: 978-988-17012-3-7).
http://hdl.handle.net/2123/2664

Kasikowski, T, et al. Cleaner production in the ammonia–soda industry: an ecological and economic study. Journal of Environmental Management, 2004, 73(4), pp 339-356.
http://dx.doi.org/10.1016/j.jenvman.2004.08.001

Keith, DW, et al. Climate Strategy with CO2 Capture from the Air. Climatic Change, 2006, 74(1-3), pp 17-45. doi: 10.1007/s10584-005-9026-x.

Keith, DW. Why Capture CO2 From the Atmosphere. Science, 2009, 325, pp 1654-55. doi: 10.1126/science.1175680

Lackner, K. Carbonate Chemistry for Sequestering Fossil Carbon. Annual Review of Energy and Environment, 2002, 27, pp 193-232. doi:10.1146/annurev.energy.27.122001.083433

Lee, JW and Li, R. Integration of fossil energy systems with CO2 sequestration through NH4HCO3 production. Energy Conversion and Management, 2002, 44, pp. 1535-1546. doi:10.1016/S0196-8904(02)00149-8

Levine, RB; Pinnarat T; Savage PE. Biodiesel Production from Wet Algal Biomass through in Situ Lipid Hydrolysis and Supercritical Transesterification.

Energy & Fuels 2010 24 (9), 5235-5243. doi: 10.1021/ef1008314

Lemmens, B, et al. Assessment of Plasma Gasification of High Caloric Waste Streams. Journal of Waste Management, 2006, 27(2007) pp 1562-1569. http://dx.doi.org/10.1016/ j.wasman.2006.07.027

Lomborg, B. "Global Warming" pp. 258-326 in The Skeptical Environmentalist. Twelfth Reprint, Cambridge University Press, 2004.

Meneses, M, et al. Alternatives for Reducing The Environmental Impact of the Main Residue From a Desalination Plant. Journal of Industrial Ecology, 2010, 14 (3), 512-527. doi: 10.1111/j.1530-9290.2010.00225.x

Meridian International Research. "The Trouble With Lithium". May, 28, 2008. http://www.meridian-int-res.com/Projects/Lithium_Microscope.pdf

Mimura, T, et al. Development of energy saving technology for flue gas Carbon Dioxide recovery in power plant by chemical absorption method and steam system. Energy Conversion and Management. 1997, 38(Supp. 1), pp S57-S62, http://dx.doi.org/10.1016/S0196-8904(96)00246-4

National Renewable Energy Laboratory, Gridley Ethanol Demonstration Project Utilizing Biomass Gasification Technology: Pilot Plant Gasifier and

Syngas Conversion Testing. 2005. http://www.nrel.gov/docs/fy05osti/37581.pdf

Pacala, S and Socolow, R. Stabilization Wedges: Solving the Climate Problem for the Next 50 Years with Current Technologies. Science, 2004, 305(5686), pp 968-972. doi: 10.1126/science.1100103

Packer, M. Algal Capture of Carbon Dioxide; Biomass Generation As a Tool for Greenhouse Gas Mitigation with Reference to New Zealand Energy Strategy and Policy. Energy Policy, 2009, 37(2009) pp 3428-3437. doi: 10.1016/ j.enpol.2008.12.025

Rau, GH and Caldeira, K. Enhanced carbonate dissolution: A means of sequestering waste CO2 as ocean bicarbonate. Energy Conversion and Management, 1999, 40: 1803–1813. doi:10.1016/S0196-8904(99)00071-0

Roesijadi, G, et al. Techno-Economic Feasibility Analysis of Offshore Seaweed Farming for Bioenergy and Biobased Products, Batelle Pacific Northwest Division, 2008, http://www.scribd.com/doc/16595766/Seaweed-Feasibility-Final-Report.

Royal Society, Geo-engineering the Climate. September 2009. http://royalsociety.org/displaypagedoc.asp?id=35094

Scholz, F and Hasse, U. Permanent Wood Sequestration: The Solution to the Global Carbon Dioxide Problem. ChemSusChem, April 8, 2008. Volume 1, Issue 5, Pp. 381-384. doi: 10.1002/cssc.200800048

Sheehan, J, et al. A Look Back at the U.S. Department of Energy's Aquatic Species Program— Biodiesel From Algae. National Renewable Energy Laboratory, 1998.
http://www1.eere.energy.gov/biomass/pdfs/biodiesel_from_algae.pdf

Sherman, SR. Nuclear Powered CO2 Capture From the Atmosphere. Environmental Progress & Sustainable Energy, 2009, 28(1), pp. 52-59. doi: 10.1002/ep.10337

Steinhauser, G. Cleaner production in the Solvay Process: general strategies and recent developments. Journal of Cleaner Production, 2008, 16(7), pp 833-841. http://dx.doi.org/10.1016/j.jclepro.2007.04.005

Stephens, JC and Keith, DW. Assessing geochemical carbon management. Climatic Change, 2008, 90, pp. 217-242. doi: 10.1007/s10584-008-9440-y

Strand, SE and Benford, G. Ocean Sequestration of Crop Residue Carbon: Recycling Fossil Fuel Carbon Back to Deep Sediments. Environ. Sci. Technol., 2009, 43 (4), pp 1000–1007. doi. 10.1021/es8015556

United States Department of Energy, Advanced Research Projects Agency- Energy, "Electro Fuels Projects: Biofuels From CO2 Using Ammonia-Oxidizing Bacteria in a Reverse Microbial Fuel Cell", 2010. http://arpa-e.energy.gov/ProgramsProjects/Electrofuels/BiofuelsfromCO2UsingAmmoniaOxidizingBacteria.aspx,

Whitty, KJ, at al. Emissions from Syngas Combustion. Combustion Science and Technology, 2008, 180(6), pp 1117-1136. http://dx.doi.org/10.1080/00102200801963326

Womack, RK. Using the Centrifugal Method for the Plasma-Arc Vitrification of Waste. JOM, 51 (10) (1999), pp. 14–16. http://www.tms.org/pubs/journals/JOM/9910/Womack-9910.html

Zeman, F. Energy and Material Balance of CO_2 Capture from Ambient Air. Environ. Sci. Technol., 2007, 41 (21), pp 7558–7563. doi: 10.1021/es070874m

Zeman, F. Experimental Results for Capturing CO_2 from the Atmosphere. AIChE Journal, 2008, 54(5), pp 1396-1399. doi: 10.1002/aic.11452

Sustainable Global Change Infrastructure (SGC-I)

TABLES AND FIGURES

Table 1 : <u>Prior Modes and Strategies for Carbon Capture and Sequestration</u>

TYPE	EXAMPLE
Flue Gas CO_2 Capture (chemical methods)	*Rochelle, GT, 2009, Amine Scrubbing for CO_2 Capture. Science, 325, pp. 1652-1654. New York, NY, doi:10.1126/science.1176731*
Flue Gas CO_2 Capture (biological methods)	*National Renewable Energy Laboratory, 2001. Microalgae Production from Power Plant Flue Gas. Pp. 15-17, Golden, Colorado. http://nrel.gov/docs/fy01osti/29417.pdf*
Coal Gasification w/CO_2 Capture	*FutureGen Alliance, 2010. FutureGen Technology, Washington, DC. http://www.futuregenalliance.org/technology.stm*
Atmospheric CO_2 Capture (chemical)	*Zeman, F, 2008. Experimental results for Capturing CO_2 from the Atmosphere, AIChE Journal 54(5), pp 1396-1399, New York, NY. Doi: 10.1002/aie.11452*
Enhanced Oil Recovery Sequestration	*Science Magazine (2009) "Carbon Sequestration", [Description of 12 Major Projects Worldwide], 325, pp. 1644-45, New York, NY.*

TYPE	EXAMPLE
Geological Sequestration	*National Energy Technology Laboratory, 2010, Carbon Sequestration Storage, Washington, DC. http://www.netl.doe.gov/technologies/carbon_seq/core_rd/stroage.html*
Mineral Sequestration	*Lackmer, K. 2002, Carbonate Chemistry for Sequestering Fossil Carbon. Ann. Review of Energy and Environment, 27, pp. 193-232. Palo Alto, CA doi:10-1146/annurev.energy.27.122001.083433*
Ocean Sequestration (direct injection)	*Caldeira, K. et.al. 2001. Predicting and evaluating the effectiveness of ocean carbon sequestration by direct injection. First National Conference on Carbon Sequestration, Washington, DC. www.netl.doe.gov/publications/proceedings/01/carbon_seq/p48.pdf*
Ocean Sequestration (deep sea sediments)	*House, KZ, et.al. 2006 Permanent carbon dioxide storage in deep-sea-sediments. PNAS, 103(33), Abstract, pp. 12291. Washington, DC. doi:10.1073/pnas.0605318103*
Biochar Sequestration	*Roberts, KG, et. Al. 2010. Life Cycle Assessment of Biochar Systems: Estimating the Energetic, Economic, and Climate Change Potential. Environmental Science & Technology, 44(2). Abstract p.827. Washington DC. doi:10.1021/es902266r*
Biomass CCS	*Scholz, F. et.al. 2008. Permanent Wood Sequestration: The Solution to the Global Carbon Dioxide Problem. ChemSusChem, April 8, Volume I, Issue 5, Abstract, pp. 381. Weinheim, Germany. doi:10.1002/cssc.20080048*

TYPE	EXAMPLE
Soil CCS	*Sundquist, ET, et.al. 2009. Rapid assessment of U.S. forest and soil organic carbon storage and forest biomass carbon sequestration capacity: U.S. Geological Survey Open-File Report 2009-1283. Abstract Washington. DC. http://pubs.usgs.gov/of/2009/1283*
Carbonate Weathering CCS (flue gas)	*Rau. G. 2008, Altering Seawater Chemistry to Mitigate CO_2 and Ocean Acidification. 5th Annual California Climate Change Conference, Sacramento, CA http://image.xyvy.info/GregRau.pdf*
Carbonate Weather CCS (atmospheric)	*House, KZ. el.al. 2007. Eletrochemical acceleration of Chemical Weathering as an Energetically Feasible Approach to Mitigating Anthropogenic Climate Change. Environmental Science & Technology, 41(24), Abstract, pp. 8464, Washington, DC, doi:10.1021/es0701816*
Ocean Nourishment CCS	*Jones, ISF, et.al. 2003. Long-term ocean carbon sequestration with macronutrient addition. Engineering Carbon Sequestration in the Ocean. Second Annual Conference on Carbon Sequestration, Washington, DC. http://www.netl.doe.gov/publications.proceedings/03.carbon-seq/PDFs/110.pdf*
Ocean Fertilization CCS	*Blain, S. et.al. 2007. Effect of natural iron fertilization on carbon sequestration in the Southern Ocean. Nature, 446, Letter. p.1070. New York, NY, doi.10.1038/nature05700*

Figures

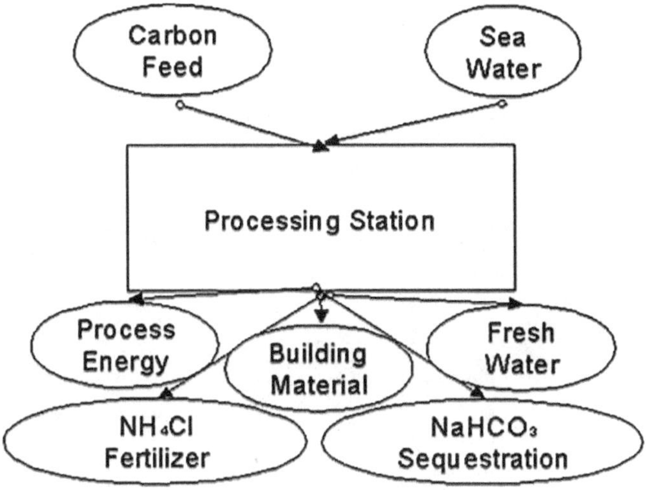

FIG. 1

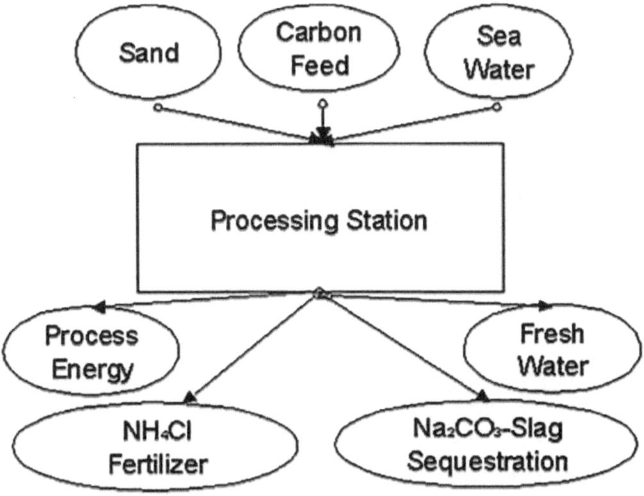

FIG. 2

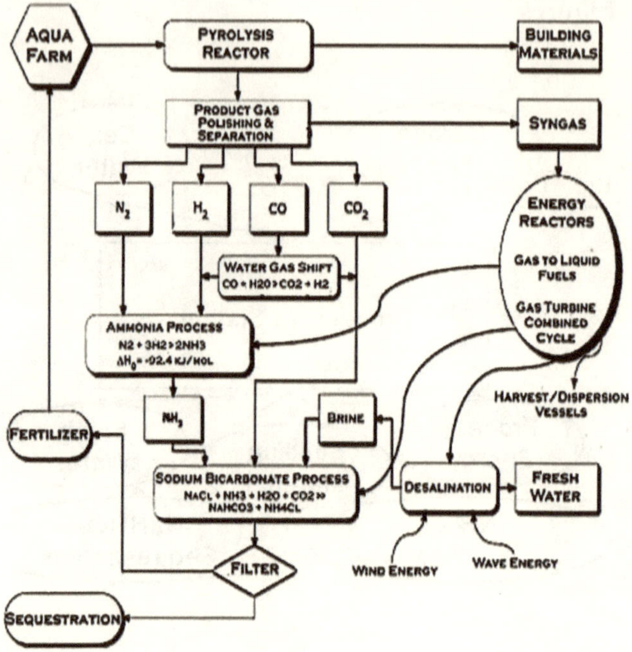
AQUA FARM
PYROLYSIS REACTOR
BUILDING MATERIALS
PRODUCT GAS POLISHING & SEPARATION
SYNGAS
N2
H2
CO
CO2
ENERGY REACTORS
GAS TO LIQUID FUELS
GAS TURBINE COMBINED CYCLE
WATER GAS SHIFT
CO + H20 > CO2 + H2
AMMONIA PROCESS
N2 + 3H2 > 2NH3
ΔH0 = -92.4 KJ/MOL
HARVEST/DISPERSION VESSELS
NH3
BRINE
FERTILIZER
SODIUM BICARBONATE PROCESS
NACL + NH3 + H20 + CO2 >>
NAHCO3 + NH4CL
DESALINATION
FRESH WATER
FILTER
WIND ENERGY
WAVE ENERGY
SEQUESTRATION

FIG. 3

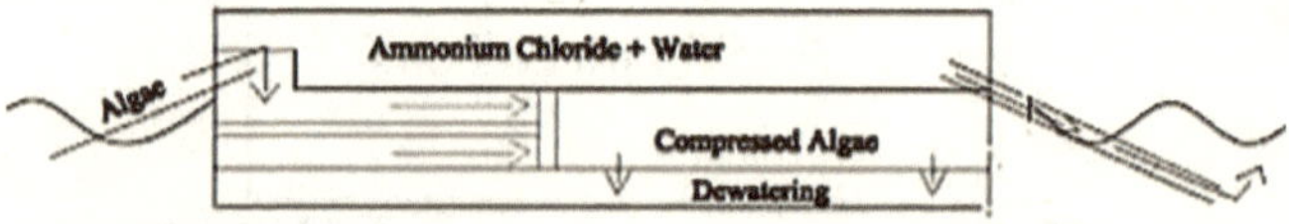
Ammonium Chloride + Water
Algae
Compressed Algae
Dewatering

FIG. 4

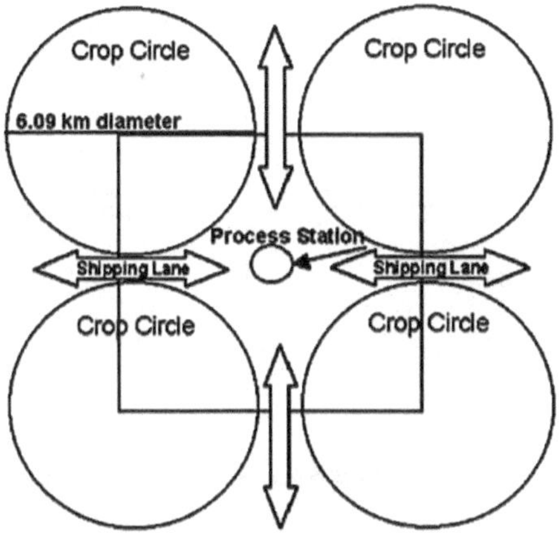
Crop Circle
Crop Circle
6.09 km diameter
Process Station
Shipping Lane
Shipping Lane
Crop Circle
Crop Circle

FIG. 5

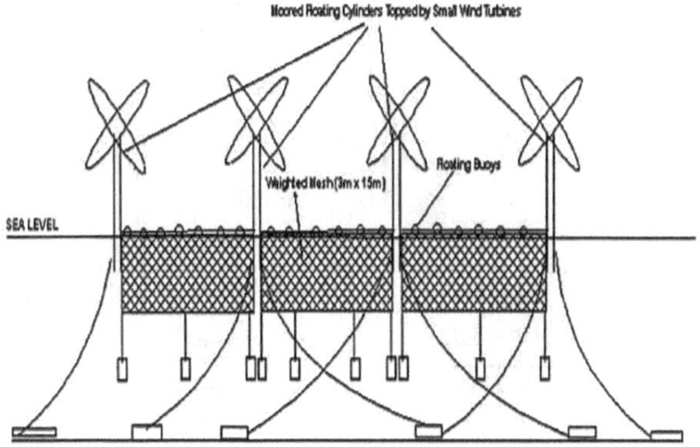
Moored Floating Cylinders Topped by Small Wind Turbines
Floating Buoys
Weighted Mesh (3m x 15m)
SEA LEVEL

FIG. 6

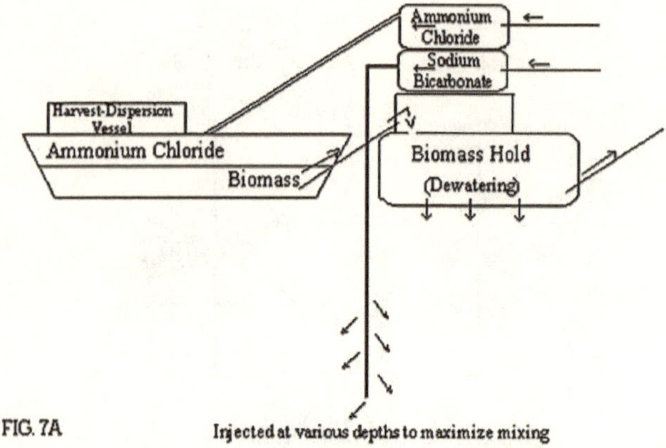
Ammonium Chloride
Sodium Bicarbonate
Harvest-Dispersion Vessel
Ammonium Chloride
Biomass
Biomass Hold
(Dewatering)
Injected at various depths to maximize mixing

FIG. 7A

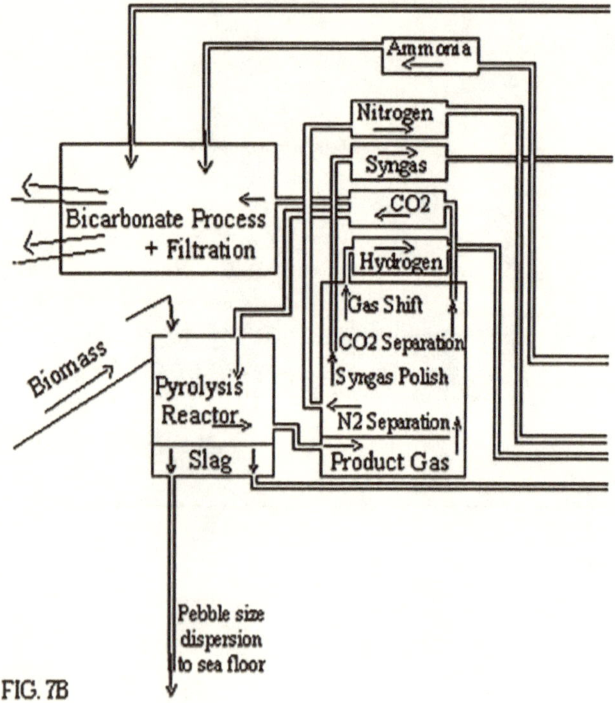
Ammonia
Nitrogen
Syngas
CO2
Hydrogen
Bicarbonate Process
+ Filtration
Gas Shift
CO2 Separation
Syngas Polish
N2 Separation
Product Gas
Biomass
Pyrolysis Reactor
Slag
Pebble size dispersion to sea floor

FIG. 7B

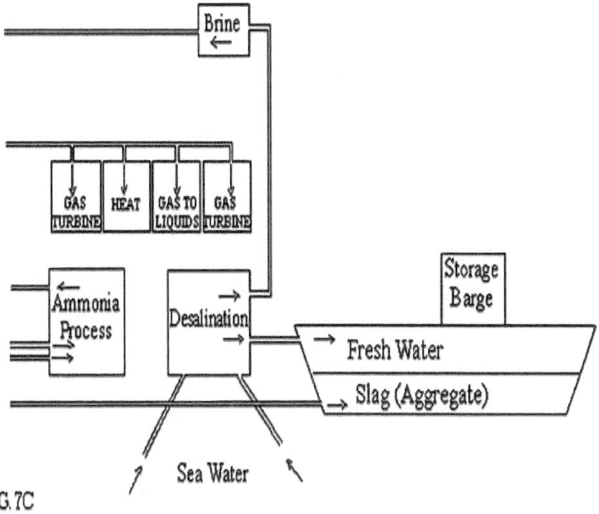
Brine
GAS TURBINE
HEAT
GAS TO LIQUIDS
GAS TURBINE
Ammonia Process
Desalination
Storage Barge
Fresh Water
Slag (Aggregate)
Sea Water

FIG. 7C

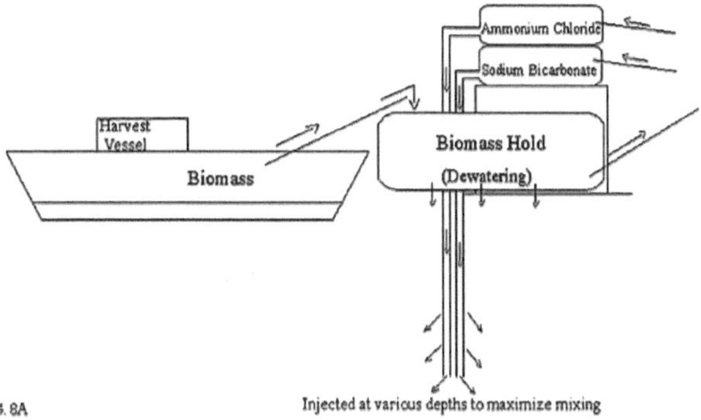
Ammonium Chloride
Sodium Bicarbonate
Harvest Vessel
Biomass
Biomass Hold
(Dewatering)
Injected at various depths to maximize mixing

FIG. 8A

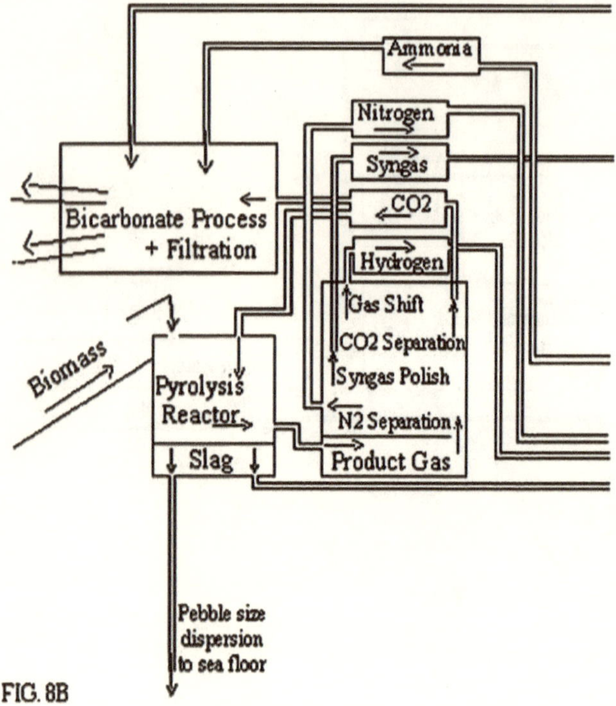
Ammonia
Nitrogen
Syngas
CO2
Hydrogen
Bicarbonate Process
+ Filtration
Gas Shift
CO2 Separation
Syngas Polish
N2 Separation
Product Gas
Biomass
Pyrolysis
Reactor
Slag
Pebble size
dispersion
to sea floor

FIG. 8B

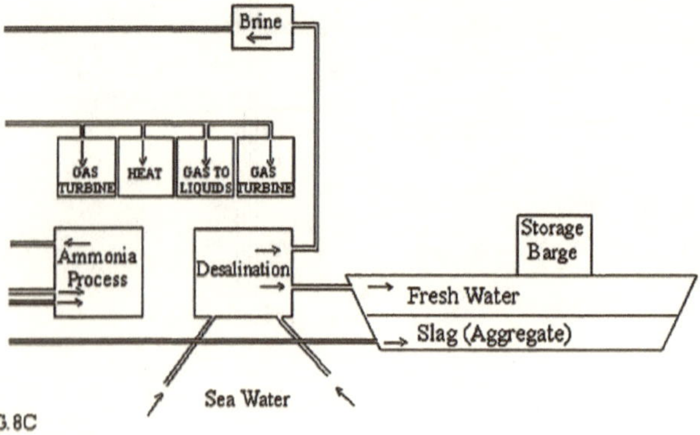
Brine
GAS TURBINE
HEAT
GAS TO LIQUIDS
GAS TURBINE
Ammonia
Process
Desalination
Storage
Barge
Fresh Water
Slag (Aggregate)
Sea Water

FIG. 8C

PUTTING FREE CAPITAL MARKETS TO WORK FOR THE ENVIRONMENT

Project: Visionvest List of Environmentally Sustainable Companies

Entrepreneurial Platform(s): Wordpress, Skype, Team Viewer

Submitted: 10/5/2010 and thereafter

Background and Description

International capital markets must be acknowledged as one of the most powerful change engines around. The amazing ability of corporations to develop, market, and distribute products has been at the root of so much innovation in the US and elsewhere. For the cleantech economy to succeed, the power of these markets cannot be ignored. This project began when I gathered together a formidable group of environmentalists with a wide range of expertise, all graduates of the Environmental Science and Policy masters program at Columbia, and all with full-time jobs. We formed an investment club and assumed the legal organization of a general partnership. Since our members lived everywhere from California to Germany to Mexico, we established an online office using a Wordpress infoblog, a Skype network, and Team Viewer capabilities. Our weekly meetings were international events with members participating from all corners of the globe. For a period of over a year, and by means of much private blogging and shared desktop viewing, we developed a list of criteria with which to evaluate companies along the lines of environmental sustainability. Then we applied these criteria to any company submitted by any member. We tested our decisions using an online broker. Over time we developed a strong analytical system and built up a solid group of companies numbering more than 250.

Although the group dissolved due to time constraints, I have continued to operate the venture independently since then, opening up this research to subscribers. I maintain continuously a list of approved companies and review and revise the list regularly. The Visionvest environmental sustainability recommendations are not a substitute for financial due diligence, nor should they be viewed as investment advice. They are a brief justification for investment in selected publicly traded companies on the grounds of environmental sustainability (http://gcorptour.wordpress.com/).

Environmentally responsible investing means investing in companies whose products or services further the environmental health of the Earth. Simply put these are companies whose activities are expected to contribute in some way to cleaner air, cleaner water, cleaner soil, safer food, healthier wildlife, and the continuing availability of natural resources and services, not only for us but also for future generations. This is the prescription for all Visionvest analysis and consists of two primary principles: 1) environmental sustainability, and 2) the precautionary principle. Environmental sustainability is most simply the ability of the natural environment to maintain its processes and functions, biological diversity, and productivity over time. According to the precautionary principle, when reasonable scientific evidence of any kind gives us good reason to believe that an activity, technology or substance may be harmful, we should act to prevent or avoid that harm. The application of these broad principles to investing requires a knowledge of environmental science, technology, engineering, policy, finance, law, and psychology.

URBAN PLANNING FOR THE MEGACITY

Project: PlaNYC 2030 Update for 2011
Entrepreneurial Platform(s): Environmental Law Committee of the New York City Bar Association, Huddle, PDF Document Exchange
Submitted: 12/22/2010

Background

The City is required by law to update the PlaNYC 2030 every four years (the PlaNYC is a long term environmental plan for the City). The first quadrennial update became April 22, 2011 and our bar association sub-committee was charged with producing a set of law and policy recommendations in the spirit of community involvement and decision making. The recommendations are organized according to the following headings: energy related, built environment related, water related, and waste related aspects of the Plan. I headed a sub-committee of the New York City Bar's Environmental Law Committee and was the chief writer of the report: I authored most of the recommendations. The report was submitted to the Mayor's Office of Long-Term Planning and Sustainability and also appears on the New York City Bar Association's portal.[3]

PlaNYC 2030 Update: 2011

Recommendations from the New York City Bar Environmental Law Committee

SUMMARY TABLE

SUBJECT AREA	**PROPOSED INITIATIVE (page#)**	**IMPLEMENTATION MILESTONE**
PlaNYC	Create Implementation Oversight Office (p.3)	Appointment of PlaNYC Oversight Officer
PlaNYC Governance	Expand Performance Metrics to Include Embedded Impacts of Products Imported into and Consumed in New York City (p.3)	Creation of embedded impacts database and data acquisition for database, summary of data in annual progress reports.
Housing	Incorporate Assorted Low Cost Energy Efficient Practices into Building Codes (p.13)	Introduce and Support Building Code Legislation
Open Space	Utilize food scrap compost for City green spaces (p.11)	Introduction of food scrap composting law to City Council for consideration

SUBJECT AREA	PROPOSED INITIATIVE (page#)	IMPLEMENTATI ON MILESTONE
Water Quality	Implement Assorted Low Cost Stromwater Reduction Practices (p.13)	Create pilot programs in furtherance of stromwater reduction practices
Water Quality	Commission Testing study of Emerging Pollutants in Treated Wastewater, Define Treatment Priorities and Options (p.19)	Publication of emerging pollutants study
Water Quality	Design a CSO Reduction Plan Driven by Sector-by-Sector Data (p.19)	Completion of CSO reduction plan for New York City
Water Quality	Package of Incentives Aimed at Reducing CSO inputs from the Private Sector (p.17)	Introduction of CSO incentive package to City Council
Water Quality	Create Clean Water Action Days Program (p.18)	Implementation of Clean Water Action Days Program
Water Network	Implement Assorted Low Cost Water Efficiency and Reduction Practices (p.13)	Create pilot programs in furtherance of water efficiency and reduction practices

SUBJECT AREA	PROPOSED INITIATIVE (page#)	IMPLEMENTATION MILESTONE
Transportation	Improve Subway Station Climate Comfort (p.8)	Select first station for demonstration project and install geothermal heating and cooling in the station.
Transportation	Create Network of Bicycle Friendly Subway Stations and Bus Pick-Up Points (p.8)	Plan system and build first pilot locations
Transportation	Implement Alternate Forms of Congestion Reducing Incentives (p.9)	Implement congestion measures and monitor improvements.
Transportation	Launch GreenRoads Program to Lessen Environmental Impact of Roadway and Sidewalk Engineering and Materials (p.10)	Publication of PlaNYC Best Practices and Materials for NYC Roadways and Sidewalks.
Transportation	Use GPS Feeds to Provide Real Time Congestion Information to Drivers and to Make Traffic Signals Responsive to Congestion (p.10)	Request for proposals from traffic engineering firms.

SUBJECT AREA	PROPOSED INITIATIVE (page#)	IMPLEMENTATI ON MILESTONE
Energy	Launch a Renewable Energy Development Plan for New York City (p.2)	Definition of Renewable Energy Target for New York City
Energy	Promote Investment Stimulating Mechanisms for Renewable Energy (p.2)	Creation of Entity with requisite Authority
Energy	Develop Additional Financing Resources for Renewable Energy Installation (p.3)	Implementation of Renewable Energy Financing Instruments
Energy	Explore EnergyShed Concept (p.4)	Publication of a technical-economic study of EnergyShed program
Energy	Pilot more non-incinerating technologies for producing waste-to-energy, including liquid fuels, gas, and heat producing technologies (p.4)	Request for small scale pilot proposals in a variety of waste-to-energy technologies.

SUBJECT AREA	PROPOSED INITIATIVE (page#)	IMPLEMENTATI ON MILESTONE
Energy	Commission a Technical-Economic Study of Offshore Hyrokinetic Energy Potentials for New York City (p.5)	Publication of a technical-economic study of hydrokinetic energy
Energy	Facilitate Expansion of Alternative Fueling Infrastructure for Private Vehicles (p.6)	Pilot program for alternative fueling availability in key metropolitan areas
Energy	Launch Program to Expand Use of Geothermal Ground Source Heat in Single and Multi-Family Dwellings (p.7)	Operation of a neighborhood pilot program to install the technology in 100 residential homes.
Energy	Accelerate Energy Efficiency Innovation (p.7)	Create the Energy Efficiency Research, Development, and Demonstration Program and begin to accept application for product research, development and demonstration start-up financing.

SUBJECT AREA	PROPOSED INITIATIVE (page#)	IMPLEMENTATI ON MILESTONE
Energy	Advanced Thermostat Controls For Residential Building Sub-Spaces (p.9)	Commission a feasibility study for various heating and cooling technologies in place in City buildings, define best practices and design and implementation plan.
Energy	Launch GreenRoads Program to Lessen Energy Footprint of Roadway and Sidewalk Engineering and Materials (p.10)	Publication of PlaNYC Best Pracices and Materials for NYC Roadways and Sidewalks
Energy	Begin implementation of real-time pricing (RTP) across the city. (p.12)	Ten percent (10%) of eligible buildings convert to RTP
Energy	Incorporate Assorted Low Cost Energy Efficient Practices into Energy Code (p.14)	Introduce and Support Energy Code Legislation

SUBJECT AREA	PROPOSED INITIATIVE (page#)	IMPLEMENTATI ON MILESTONE
Air Quality	Ramp up biofuel use in the City's truck and vehicle fleets, beginning with the conversion of all City school busses to 100% biofuels (p.6)	Set a specific targets for biofuel conversion
Air Quality	Create new programs to expand electric vehicle and hybrid electric vehicle development in the New York City taxi and limousine fleet (p.6)	50% of the New York City taxi fleet consists of at least hybrid electric vehicles.
Air Quality	Decrease Toxic Emissions from Building Materials (p.15)	Introduce and Support Building Code-Legislation Requiring the Use of Low Toxic Emissions Materials.
Climate Change	Launch and Eco-Labeling Program for Products Sold in New York City (p.12)	Commission techno-feasibility study of eco-labeling for products sold in New York City.

SUBJECT AREA	PROPOSED INITIATIVE (page#)	IMPLEMENTATI ON MILESTONE
Waste Management	New Scope of Action Category (p.18)	Inclusion of Waste Management as Major Impact and Initiative Category in all PlaNYC Planning and Reports
Waste Management	Create Solid Waste Reduction Intergovernmental Task Force for New York City (p.18)	Commission a comprehensive study of solid waste reduction strategies available to New York City
Waste Management	Develop Mechanism for Variable Waste Pricing (p.11)	Commission preliminary Feasibility Study of Solid Waste Reduction via Alternative Pricing Mechanisms and Collection Technologies.
Waste Management	Create feasible food scrap composting program, including collection and utilization of compost for City green spaces (p.11)	Introduction of food scrap composting law to City Council for consideration.

SUBJECT AREA	PROPOSED INITIATIVE (page#)	IMPLEMENTATI ON MILESTONE
GreeNYC	Expand Public Involvement in Ideating and Monitoring of PlaNYC Policies, Goals, Initiatives, and Milestones (p.8)	Re-design PlaNYC website to include individual subject area pages where public participation is an essential part of PlaNYC implementation; Development of PlaNYC-Tech Center concept.

Background

The City is required by law (Local Law 17 of 2008) to update PlaNYC 2030 every four years. The first quadrennial update is due April 22, 2011. The Mayor's Office of Long-Term Planning and Sustainability is leading the effort to update the plan, and as part of this effort, the City has created several ways for New Yorkers to take part in a citywide conversation on PlaNYC 2030. This set of law and policy recommendations from the New York City Bar's Environmental Law Committee is offered in the spirit of community involvement and we respectfully request that the following be considered, where appropriate, by the Mayor's Office of Long-Term Planning and Sustainability. The recommendations are organized according to the following headings:

energy related (p.5), built environment related (p.16), water related (p.20), and waste related (p. 22) aspects of the Plan. In cases where an entry addresses an already ongoing program, the recommendation is to formally incorporate the program into the PlaNYC's slate of initiatives.

ENERGY
Related Recommendations

1. Renewable Energy

The New York State Renewable Energy Assessment of December 2009 concludes that New York's renewable energy technical potential is approximately 90 percent of the 2018 forecasted electricity generation requirement.[4] New York State also possesses considerable biomass resources that could be used to produce bio-oils.[5] In New York City, energy prices have stayed 40% higher than the national average for the past 5 years.[6] Since most energy analysts expect the prices of fossil fuels to continue to increase even more during the coming years, if only from the perspective of reducing energy costs[7], the State and New York City stand to benefit from an expansion of renewable energy use. Furthermore, the New York State Renewable Portfolio Standard targets 30% of the State's electricity to come from renewable sources by 2015 and has recently instituted a program aimed at encouraging geographic balance (very few, if any, RPS projects are located in or around New York City). The main thrust of the following recommendations is to bridge the gap between New York City's current renewable energy portfolio, including non-electricity fuels, and the New York State RPS program. Gains in renewable energy consumption by New York City are likely to have beneficial effects in other PlaNYC areas such as transportation, air quality, and climate change.

A. Governance and Finance

i) New York State is currently operating under the 2002 Renewable Portfolio Standard for electricity generation, as updated periodically. New York City currently has no similar renewable energy target. The New York City Energy Planning Board should develop a Renewable Energy Development Plan specifically tailored for New York City, including mechanisms for financing projects in furtherance of the plan (see recommendations 1.A.ii and 1.A.iii, below). This plan should devise a reasonable target for renewable energy consumption in New York City, either produced locally or imported, should not increase the RPS cost burden to utility customers, and should include technologies appropriate for New York City (such as municipal waste biomass, small scale geothermal, biomass to liquids, and hydrokinetic production-- in addition to the renewable sources defined in the State RPS). The Plan may also consider the creation of an EnergyShed program (see recommendation 1.B.i, below).

a) Current Energy Initiative On Point: None

b) Updated Energy Initiative: #11.v– Launch a Renewable Energy Development Plan for New York City

c) New Implementation Milestone: Definition of Renewable Energy Target for New York City

ii) In the area of long-term city-wide renewable energy supply, there is a growing consensus that an effective long-term renewable energy policy requires the creation of an institutional mechanism capable of stimulating additional, high-risk investments into that particular type of energy infrastructure. Worldwide, the value of fossil fuel subsidies exceeds those for renewable energy by about 12 to1,[8] creating a large global gap in renewable energy financing. Clean Renewable Energy Bonds (CREBS), loan guarantees, and power purchase agreements are but three examples of policy instruments that could be stimulated to overcome the large risks taken by renewable energy investors. The principle has been recognized not only in the original PlaNYC document, but also by the ad-hoc NYC Energy Planning Board, and in the 2010 PlaNYC Progress Report. The ELC recommends that an appropriate mechanism be instituted whereby the City of New York may provide sufficient incentives to expand renewable energy supply to New York City.

a) Current Energy Initiative On Point: None

b) Updated Energy Initiative: #11.w– Promote Investment Stimulating Mechanisms for Renewable Energy

c) New Implementation Milestone: Creation of an entity with authority to initiate and guarantee long-term clean power supply and infrastructure contracts and to facilitate renewable energy bond formation.

iii) In the area of financing for renewable energies, it is apparent that New York City will require its fair share of State RPS funding as well as the use of creative policy instruments to bridge the gap between market-based strategies and the goals of PlaNYC. The ELC recommend that the New York City Energy Planning Board be authorized to advocate before all appropriate bodies for an equitable distribution of RPS funding in addition to those funds already obtained (based on prior PlaNYC documents there appears to be a $145 Million shortfall in RPS funding incentives for the City) and that the appropriate city agencies be authorized to expand the use of additional measures such as Property Assessed Clean Energy (PACE)[9] financing and energy aligned leases[10] in New York City.

a) Current Energy Initiative On Point: None

b) Updated Energy Initiative: #11.x– Develop Additional Financing Resources for Renewable Energy Installation

c) New Implementation Milestones: Agreement on additional RPS funding; Implementation of Renewable Energy Financing Instruments

iv) PlaNYC is a game-plan for sustainability composed of numerous initiatives and programs. As with all policy directives, there is always the possibility that written concepts fail to materialize upon implementation. One example of this occurs when 'green' criteria contained in requests for proposals do not survive into the contracting phase.[11] Another example could be where clean electricity generation fees paid by ratepayers are not applied to the generation of new, clean electricity (in other words, making sure that each dollar paid for clean energy is actually being used to generate an additional unit of clean energy). The ECL recommends the creation of a PlaNYC Oversight Officer within the Office of Long-Term Planning and Sustainability to oversee the proper execution on the ground of PlaNYC initiatives.

a) Current PlaNYC Initiative On Point: None

b) Updated PlaNYC Initiative: #1– Create PlaNYC Implementation Oversight Office

c) New Implementation Milestones:Establishment of post of PlaNYC Oversight Officer and commencement of oversight functions

v) An expansion of PlaNYC metrics and progress statistics would produce even stronger and more accurate results in many of the broad categories. The most obvious of these is the renewable energy utilization metric. Another very important metric that is lacking in the current version of PlaNYC concerns the environmental impacts of products imported from outside the City for use or consumption within the City. To give but just one example, a food item, such as a box of cereal, contains a certain amount of embedded energy, represents a certain amount of water use, of pesticide use, carbon emissions, and so on. A true representation of New York City's environmental impact must include the impacts of imported products (this includes comestibles, construction materials, discretionary items, etc). PlaNYC should expand its air quality, energy, climate change, and water metrics to include the impacts within these categories of products produced elsewhere but consumed within New York City (see also recommendation 2.F.i, below).

a) Current PlaNYC Initiative On Point: None

b) Updated PlaNYC Initiative: #2– Expand PlaNYC Performance Metrics to Include Embedded Impacts of Products Imported into and Consumed in New York City

c) New Implementation Milestones: Creation of embedded impacts database and data acquisition for database; summary of data in annual progress reports

B. Base Load Generation

i) Finding suitable sources of renewable energy strictly within the geographical (including offshore) boundaries of New York City may prove difficult. Borrowing from the successful New York City Watershed supply and protection system, the proposed New York City Renewable Energy Development Plan (see recommendation 1, above) could include consideration of a New York City EnergyShed system. The basic contours of such a system could include the creation of a supply network of renewable energy crops and resources in the downstate area, the installation of a production infrastructure for these resources, the installation of a transmission and delivery system from these areas to New York City (possibly using current aqueduct routes), and the conversion of these energies into commodities for distribution to New York City consumers. Among the many benefits of an EnergyShed system would be the development of a biocrop economy for New York State's farmers and landowners, the replacement of residual heating oils with bio-oils, and the substitution of biodiesel in school buses, waste collection trucks, and other city-operated diesel vehicles and equipment.

a) Current Energy Initiative On Point: None

b) Updated Energy Initiative: #15– Explore EnergyShed Program

c) New Implementation Milestones: Publication of a technical-economic study of EnergyShed Concept

ii) The ability to sponsor smaller scale pilot demonstrations of new technologies is one of New York City's surest paths to energy innovation. The current PlaNYC includes an initiative to pilot non-incinerating waste-to-energy technologies that should receive continued and expanded support, including an exploration of energy waste collection and sorting modalities and processing sites (including offshore processing) . In addition to the anaerobic digester and waste-chip boiler highlighted in the 2010 Progress Report, the City should encourage pilot plants able to convert municipal wastes, sewage solids, Parks Department waste, and other forms of waste into energy, ranging from electricity to district heat to synthetic gas to hydrogen to liquid fuels (see footnote for partial list of non-incinerating technologies).[12]

a) Current Energy Initiative On Point: #11.6– Pilot one or more technologies for producing energy from solid waste

b) Updated Energy Initiative: #11.6– Pilot more non-incinerating technologies for producing waste-to-energy, including liquid fuels, gas, and heat producing technologies

c) New Implementation Milestones: Request for small scale pilot proposals in a variety of waste-to-energy technologies.

iii) One of New York City's untapped and plentiful renewable energy resources is offshore hydrokinetic. Various technologies such as wave energy converters and current converters are being piloted throughout the world. Some are being co-located with wind turbines. The first step towards harnessing this energy source is to assess it potential. For this purpose, the City should commission a technical-economic study of offshore hydrokinetic technologies as a preliminary step towards possible further application of these technologies.

a) Current Energy Initiative On Point: None

b)Updated Energy Initiative: #11.y– Commission a Technical-Economic Study of Offshore Hydrokinetic Energy Potentials for New York City

c) New Implementation Milestones: Publication of a technical-economic study of Hydrokinetic energy

C. On-Site and Mobile Combustion

i) Quite a few alternative fuel vehicles are now available on the market, both from domestic and foreign sources. An initial obstacle to the wider adoption of these vehicles is the availability of an alternative fueling infrastructure. The US Department of Energy has made available a database of alternative fueling stations that makes evident the lack of publicly accessible facilities in and around New York City.[13]

A coherent strategy for this infrastructure should be initiated under the auspices of PlaNYC. Among the options for consideration are availability of EV and HEV charging stations in parking garages, the availability of ethanol, biodiesel, and other biofuels at more fueling stations, and the integration of biofuel supply with a program such as EnergyShed (see recommendation 1.B.i, above).

a) Current Energy Initiative On Point: None

b) Updated Energy Initiative: #11.z– Facilitate Expansion of Alternative Fueling Infrastructure for Private Vehicles

c) New Implementation Milestones: Pilot program for alternative fueling availability in key metropolitan areas.

ii) Some recent studies have shown that diesel emissions from school buses are especially harmful to children riding inside the buses.[14] Particulate filters are a good starting remedy, but an even more effective way of reducing harmful emissions from school buses would be to substitute more biofuels (such as biodiesel, bio-butanol, bio-methanol, and dimethyl ether) for their existing engines. Such a measure would serve a dual purpose of addressing potential children's health issues and increasing the use of renewable fuels in the City. Other city vehicles that are still using large fractions of conventional petroleum based fuels, such as waste collection trucks and fire engines, as well as City generators and equipment engines, should be shifted to an ever-increasing biofuel fraction as well. Vehicles and equipment owned by private companies that perform the same functions should be held to the same fuel substitution standards. This initiative may be productively integrated with a program such as EnergyShed (see recommendation 1.B.i, above).

a) Current Air Quality Initiative On Point: #4.1– Introduce biodiesel into the City's truck fleet, go beyond compliance with local laws, and further reduce emissions

b) Updated Air Quality Initiative: #4.1– Ramp up biofuel use in the City's truck and vehicle fleets, beginning with the conversion of all City school buses to 100% biofuels

c) New Implementation Milestones: Set specific targets for biofuel conversion

iii) The 2010 Progress Report shows that 25% of City taxicabs are now electric hybrid vehicles. PlaNYC should continue to explore ways of increasing the percentage of electricity-driven taxis and limousines. Two possible options include a program and incentives for converting conventional vehicles to hybrid electric ones, and initiating a pilot battery-swap program for electric taxis and limousines for further evaluation.

a) Current Air Quality Initiative On Point: None

b) Updated Air Quality Initiative: #3.x– Create new programs to expand electric vehicle and hybrid electric vehicle deployment in the New York City taxi and limousine fleet.

c) New Implementation Milestones: 50% of the New York City taxi fleet consists of at least hybrid electric vehicles.

iv) For New York City's large stock of single and multi-family dwellings, the option of closed-loop geothermal ground source heat for both heating and cooling represents a vast untapped reservoir of renewable energy. PlaNYC could help to unleash this potential by promoting an economic development program around this technology. Economic incentives for property owners, job training and certification for installers, and best practices advice for all parties, would lead the way towards geothermal energy use.

a) Current Energy Initiative On Point: None

b) Updated Energy Initiative: #16– Launch Program to Expand Use of Geothermal Ground Source Heat in Single and Multi-Family Dwellings

c) New Implementation Milestones: Operation of a neighborhood pilot program to install the technology in 100 residential homes.

2. Reduced Energy Consumption

A. Governance and Finance

i) Since continuing progress in reduced energy consumption depends largely on innovative efficiency strategies, technologies, and materials, then it well behooves the Plan to devise a strategy for stimulating these innovations for particular application to New York City. A key to achieving this goal may be found in the City's policy for biotechnology innovation which has been a combination of providing low-cost research facilities plus a mechanism for recognizing worthy ideas and financing early start-ups seeking to commercialize these ideas. A similar model could be applied to create an 'Energy Efficiency Research, Development, and Demonstration Program'. This program could be integrated into the PlaNYC Tech Center initiative (see recommendation 2.A.ii, below)

a) Current Energy Initiative On Point: None

b) Updated Energy Initiative: #17– Accelerate Energy Efficiency Innovation

c) New Implementation Milestones: Create the Energy Efficiency Research, Development, and Demonstration Program and begin to accept applications for product research, development, and demonstration start-up financing.

ii) According to the latest research, public participation is an essential component of successful environmental assessment and decision making[15], and policy execution[16]. Many of the goals of PlaNYC would benefit from increased public engagement. The public commenting events and systems created in conjunction with the 2011 update are good examples of public participation programs. The GreeNYC initiative is well suited to foster public involvement with PlaNYC and the ELC recommends an expansion of GreeNYC initiatives aimed at public participation throughout the inter-update period to guarantee continued positive support and results for plan initiatives. New or expanded GreeNYC programs may include monitored, public blogs on the PlaNYC website covering each of the PlaNYC areas; crowd-sourcing of ideas for new initiatives; development of online voting for crowd-sourcing ideas; and utilization of a portion of Governor's Island for a PlaNYC-Tech Center where new technology is showcased, new products are developed by professional researchers and/or citizens with prize winning ideas, and a citizen-science monitoring center are all housed.

a) Current GreeNYC Initiative On Point: None

b)Updated GreeNYC Initiative: #1– Expand Public Involvement in Ideating and Monitoring of PlaNYC Policies, Goals, Initiatives, and Milestones

c) Implementation Milestone: Re-design PlaNYC website to include individual subject area pages where public participation is an essential part of

PlaNYC implementation; Development of PlaNYC-Tech Center concept

B. Increased Use of Public Transportation

i.1) New York City is already benefiting from significant subway use as shown by the 2010 Progress Report. A tough question is how to achieve even more impressive results without altogether banning vehicles from certain areas. In this vein, there are two recommendations that could produce incremental improvements. The first is to make subway stations more climate comfortable by using the renewable resource of geothermal ground source heat to both heat and cool subway platforms in the major stations. Geothermal heating and cooling systems would prevent the sauna and ice cube effects that make platforms unsupportable during exceptionally hot and cold days, while also serving to enhance our use and knowledge of this source of energy.

a) Current Transportation Initiative On Point: None

b) Updated Transportation Initiative: #17–Improve Subway Station Climate Comfort

c) New Implementation Milestones: Select first station for demonstration project and install geothermal heating and cooling in the station.

i.2) The second recommendation to encourage subway and bus use is to make subway and bus riding more bicycle accessible by developing a program for bicycle pathways to select stations and bus pick-up points and providing bicycle parking at these select locations. While bicycles are permitted in the subways and on buses, they are not practical means of commuting during busy hours of operation. A well planned and executed system of making certain stations and pickup locations especially convenient for cyclists would help to overcome this limitation. These locations, not necessarily the busiest or largest ones, would be specially geared towards bicycle commuters by providing adjacent areas of well lit and guarded parking where a large number of riders could park their equipment safely and indefinitely. A carefully designed network of subway and bus access bicycle lanes could assure access to these stations from areas underserved by the subway and bus systems as well by means of the main system of bicycle paths already well underway. These special stations could also be the locations for a system of bicycle rentals throughout the City. If necessary, a small annual parking fee could help defray program expenses.

a) Current Transportation Initiative On Point: #9– Promote Cycling

b) Updated Transportation Initiative: #9.1– Create Network of Bicycle Friendly Subway Stations and Bus Pick-up Points

c) New Implementation Milestones: Plan system and build first pilot station

ii) The early PlaNYC experience with congestion pricing illustrates the difficult gauntlet that this type of policy must run. In spite of the brouhaha already encountered and the application of certain very good measures, the situation is still quite bad, especially for cross-town travel. There are alternative congestion strategies that could alleviate delays in the central business district by either encouraging greater use of public transportation or managing the roads more efficiently. The first of these is to increase the fees for on-street parking meters and for parking meter violations, both of which need no further explanation. The second is to increase the parking tax for garages within the central business district, which also needs no further explanation. The third is to further incentivize and make permanent an off-hours delivery program that limits the hours of freight and construction deliveries in the Central Business District to the hours between 7pm and 6am.

a) Current Transportation Initiative On Point: #10– Pilot Congestion Pricing

b) Updated Energy Initiative: #10– Implement Alternate Forms of Congestion Reducing Incentives

c) New Implementation Milestones: Implement congestion measures and monitor improvements.

C. Energy Efficiency

i) As shown in the 2010 Inventory of City Greenhouse Emissions, energy use in buildings is highly driven by exterior temperature. There are many buildings in the City where one temperature setting affects multiple levels and rooms within the building. This inefficiency can often require residents to open windows in the height of winter to prevent overheating. Therefore one fundamental peg of building efficiency is a high degree of individual responsiveness to temperature shifts, from room to room, using advanced thermostat-controlled heating and cooling. A city-wide program to convert all separately heated and cooled residential building spaces to individualized thermostat control will equate to significant gains in energy consumption, not to mention other salubrious quality of life effects.

a) Current Energy Initiative On Point: None

b) Updated Energy Initiative: #4.1– Advanced Thermostat Controls For Residential Building Sub-Spaces

c) New Implementation Milestones: Commission a feasibility study for various heating and cooling technologies in place in City buildings, define best practices, and design an implementation plan.

ii) The widespread adoption of Global Positioning System technology in passenger vehicles opens up a new avenue for increasing fuels efficiency in congested areas. Integrating vehicle GPS systems with real time CBD congestion information could be the foundation of an effective congestion management and communication network with on-screen delay advisories and alternate route suggestions made on the spot. Furthermore, computerized traffic signals could also be programmed to respond to congestion information feeds coming via GPS.

a) Current Transportation Initiative On Point: #11.2– Create an integrated traffic management system

b) Updated Transportation Initiative: #11.2– Use GPS Feeds to Provide Real Time Congestion Information to Drivers and to Make Traffic Signals Responsive to Congestion

c) New Implementation Milestones: Request for proposals from traffic engineering firms.

D. Lower Energy Materials

i) One of the major management tasks for New York City is the constant upkeep and replacement of road and sidewalk surfaces. These areas constitute a significant proportion of the City's spacial extent. Advancing the engineering practices and materials used for roads and sidewalks offers the potential of addressing a variety of PlaNYC goals such as air quality (reduced VOC and particulate emissions[17]), energy reduction (lower embedded energies, reduced maintenance[18]), vehicle efficiency (surface dynamics[19]), water quality (higher permeability[20], lower toxic run-off[21]), and climate change (higher reflectivity[22]). Due to the numerous environmental impacts of roads and sidewalks, PlaNYC should implement an advanced surfacing program to assist in the development and implementation of lower impact technologies and materials.[23]

a) Current Transportation Initiative On Point: None

b) Updated Transportation Initiative: #17–Launch GreenRoads Program to Lessen Environmental Impacts of Roadway and Sidewalk Engineering and Materials

c) New Implementation Milestones: Publication of PlaNYC Best Practices and Materials for NYC Roadways and Sidewalks

E. Waste Related Energy Reductions

i) Waste reduction has long been recognized as one of the shortest routes to environmental sustainability. However, in New York City there is no economic incentive favoring waste reduction because waste disposal pricing is not based on rate of use of the service. Persons discarding zero waste pay the same for waste disposal as heavy users. To align the economics of the waste disposal system with the policy ideals, a variable pricing mechanism based on rates is needed. This is obviously a difficult challenge and yet one that is well within the horizon of the year

2030. In order to begin the development of appropriate pricing mechanisms, PlaNYC should commission a techno-economic study that examines alternatives for assessing use-based waste disposal fees to New York City's citizens and businesses.

a) Current Waste Management Initiative On Point: None

b) Updated Waste Management Initiative: #18–Develop Mechanism for Variable Waste Pricing

c) New Implementation Milestones: Commission Preliminary Feasibility Study of Solid Waste Reduction via Alternative Pricing Mechanisms and Collection Technologies

ii) About 17% of municipal waste consists of food scraps.[24] The avoidance of this portion of the waste stream could reduce the City's annual waste stream, thereby improving energy, climate change, air quality, and cost impacts. Food scrap composting programs have been operational in Seattle and San Francisco since 2009.[25] PlaNYC should design and implement a feasible plan for food scrap composting together with a compost collection and utilization system using these other programs as a point of departure.

a) Current OpenSpace Initiative On Point: None

b) Updated OpenSpace Initiative: #7.x– Create a feasible food scrap composting program, including collection and utilization of compost for City green spaces.

c) New Implementation Milestones: Introduction of food scrap composting law to City Council for consideration

F. Consumer Choices

i) Consumer choice is an under-utilized pathway for lowering New York City's environmental impacts. In order for consumers to make purchasing choices that include environmental impact considerations, these impacts must be readily accessible. Few consumers have the time to conduct independent research on each of the products they buy so a product labeling system is necessary to convey this information and allow direct comparison at the point of purchase. An eco-labeling system for products sold in New York City could include a standardized metric for impacts such as water intensity, energy intensity, carbon intensity, and possibly others. Such information is usually already known to manufacturers and producers and could be added to existing labels without much additional cost. The eco-labeling program could be developed in conjunction with the adoption of product metrics into PlaNYC progress assessments (see Governance recommendation (v), above).

a) Current Climate Change Initiative On Point: None

b) Updated Climate Change Initiative: #4–Launch an Eco-Labeling Program for Products Sold in New York City

c) New Implementation Milestones: Commission techno-feasibility study of eco-labeling for products sold in New York City

ii) In the realm of consumer choice and citizen involvement, the establishment of variable electricity pricing could be the most cost-effective means for managing the City's power load. Furthermore, electricity consumers need to be made aware of pricing options available to them under new programs. Several initiatives are being pursued by current PlaNYC initiatives and the ELC recommends aggressive implementation of these initiatives.

a) Current Energy Initiative On Point: #6.1– Support expansion of real-time pricing (RTP) across the city.

b) Updated Energy Initiative: #6.1– Begin implementation of real-time pricing (RTP) across the city.

c) New Implementation Milestones: Ten percent (10%) of eligible buildings converted to RTP.

BUILT ENVIRONMENT
Related Recommendations

One theme running through the PlaNYC Progress Report 2010 is that fiscal constraints, whether lack of funding or lack of ability to borrow money for capital projects, have stalled some of PlaNYC's initiatives. Yet, there are a number of low-cost actions that can be taken with regard to the impact that New York City's built environment has on the natural environment, which would advance the goals of PlaNYC. The NYC Green Codes Task Force identified 111 actions that would "green" the City's building and construction codes. Many of these actions, according to the Green Codes Task Force Report[26], would have low or no cost, and still others would be of moderate cost. It is recommended that, in this time of reduced tax revenues and reduced lending, PlaNYC focus on those actions identified by the Green Codes Task Force that can be implemented without significant public fiscal impact or need for the private sector to borrow money. The following are specific recommendations from the Green Codes Task Force identified as having low or no cost, which would advance the positive impact that the built environment can have on PlaNYC's goals. The recommendations are grouped by the categories in the PlaNYC Progress Report 2010 and identified by the Green Codes Task Force designation. Please refer to the Green Codes Report for additional explanations.

1. Water Quality

Managing stormwater is identified in the PlaNYC Progress Report 2010 as the "biggest remaining challenge" (*id.* p. 30) pertaining to water quality. Most of the following actions would directly ameliorate the management of stormwater. The last is a water treatment strategy.

SW 1 – reduce excessive site paving (low cost)

SW 2 – require increased detention systems for new development (low to moderate cost)

SW 3 – regulate stormwater runoff on constructions sites smaller than one acre (moderate cost)

SW 4 – send rainwater directly to waterways (moderate cost)

SW 5 – revise stormwater regulations to account for landscape-based strategies (no cost)

SW 6 – require property owners to maintain stormwater detention systems (low cost)

HT 13 – require treatment of washwater from concrete trucks (moderate cost)

a) Current Water Quality Initiative On Point: #9–Pilot Promising Best Management Practices (BMPs)

b) Updated Water Quality Initiative: #9.x–Implement Assorted Low Cost Stormwater Reduction Practices

c) New Implementation Milestone: Create pilot programs in furtherance of stormwater reduction practices

2. Water Network

Reduction in the unnecessary use of potable water reduces demand on the City's water supply network and frees up the watershed's output for other environmental and economic uses. In October 2010, the City Council passed four local laws designed to increase water efficiency and access to potable water. Three of these laws – Int. 263/LL 54, Int. 268/LL56, and Int. 271/LL57 – implement recommendations made by the Green Codes Task Force (WE 6 – discontinue use of potable water in "once-through" cooling systems; WE 3 – submetering of water use to detect leaks quickly; and WE 1 – enhanced water efficiency standards. There are still other low and moderate cost recommendations from the Green Codes Task Force that would further reduce demand for potable water.

WE 2 – require upgrade of bathroom fixtures when bathrooms are renovated (low cost)

WE 4 – expand use of recycled water (low cost)

WE 5 – reduce use of potable water for washing sidewalks (low cost)

WE 7 – require reuse of ConEd steam condensate (moderate cost)

EE 18 – require maximization of recovery of heat from steam condensate (moderate cost)

a) Current Water Network Initiative On Point: #4 –Launch a Major New Water Conservation Effort

b) Updated Water Network Initiative: #4.x– Implement Assorted Low Cost Water Efficiency and Reduction Practices

c) New Implementation Milestone: Create pilot programs in furtherance of water efficiency and reduction practices

3 .Transportation

Please see section 2-D-i, Lower Energy Materials, in the Energy Recommendations section, above.

4. Energy

The package of four local laws passed in 2010 (47, 48, 51, and 52) that modify lighting standards to take daylight into consideration, require installation of occupancy-based and photo-sensing lighting controls in commercial buildings, and permit use of occupancy-based and photo-sensing lighting controls in public areas of residential buildings is significant progress. (*Cf.* EF 10 and EE 15 – reduce artificial lighting in sunlight spaces, EE 7 – lighting efficiency in residential buildings, and EE 13 – manual on, auto off lighting) The City's relevant agencies, including DOB and HPD, should undertake outreach to assure that the people who are on the ground making decisions about lighting are aware of what is now required and/or allowed. Organizations such as the Rent Stabilization Association, Local 32 B&J, New York Council on Coops, Federation of Coops, Association of Riverdale Coops, and BOMA are logical targets for such outreach.

The Progress Report states that the City is working to develop and pilot "energy aligned leases." (p. 57) The existence of "misaligned incentives" for efficiency upgrades in commercial buildings (*id.*) has been recognized by the private sector and model "green leases" have been developed. It is recommended that, rather than inject itself unnecessarily into contract drafting between private entities, the City, in conjunction with Con Ed, devise incentives for landlords and tenants to incorporate "energy aligned" provisions into their leases.

The following are specific actions recommended by the Green Codes Task Force that will further energy conservation at low to moderate cost.

EF 1 – make ASHRAE 90.1 the sole energy code for commercial buildings (low cost)

EF 2 – require all new residential buildings three stories or less to meet ENERGY STAR home standards (as set forth by NYSERDA in the New York ENERGY STAR Homes Technical Specifications) (low cost)

EF 4 – promote super-insulated exterior walls by excluding a significant amount of wall thickness from Floor Area calculations, thereby not penalizing a building's FAR when it uses a super-insulated exterior wall (no cost)

EF 5 – promote external insulation on existing buildings by allowing it to extend into building setbacks (no cost)

EF 6 – increase allowable size of exterior window shades (no cost)

EF 9 – DOB to require proof that residential windows open to the required minimum (low cost)

EF 11 – require cool roof coatings (low cost)

EF 12 – require cool and/or shaded building lots (low cost)

EF 13 – DOB to develop clear standards for placement of solar panels on roof tops (low cost)

EF 14 – Exempt solar panels from being counted as another "floor" of a building (low cost)

EF 15 – amend Zoning Resolution to permit alternative energy equipment on roofs (low cost)

EF 16 – amend Landmarks Law to treat alternative energy equipment the same as other mechanical equipment on roofs (low cost)

EE 3 – require developers of new large buildings to analyze possibility of cogeneration (low cost)

EE 8 – require ENERGY STAR ® appliances in newly renovated buildings and apartments (low cost)

EE 9 – require public dryers in coops, condos, and apartments to sell time in 15 minute increments (low cost)

EE 14 – limit after-hours lighting in retail spaces (low cost)

EE 20 – establish clear criteria for "sidewall venting" of boilers (low cost)

EE 21 – update boiler regulations (low cost)

EE 22 – reduce lighting power capacity requirements for offices (low cost)

EE 25 – require commissioning of new energy systems (moderate cost)

EE 26 – require testing of new lighting systems (moderate cost)

EE 28 – require boiler testing, cleaning, tuning and repairs in large buildings (low cost)

EO 3 – train building operators in energy efficiency (low cost)

EO 5 – require inspection and maintenance of commercial HVAC systems (low cost)

EO 6 – set upper limits for heating and lower limits for cooling (low cost)

a) Current Energy Initiative On Point: #3 – Strengthen Energy and Building Codes in New York City

b) Updated Energy Initiative: #3.x– Incorporate Assorted Low Cost Energy Efficiency Practices into Energy and Building Codes

c) New Implementation Milestone: Introduce and Support Building and Energy Code Legislation

5. Air Quality

The biggest outstanding concern noted in the Progress Report is small particle pollution caused by the approximately 9,900 private buildings that burn #4 and/or #6 fuel oil. The City itself, through the Department of Education, is making progress in more efficient and cleaner operation of its boilers. It is recommended that the City work with the relevant groups, including the Rent Stabilization Association, the coop groups mentioned, and the New York Oil Heating Association, to create incentives to switch to cleaner fuels and to upgrade boilers for cleaner and more efficient burning. The Green Codes Task Force addresses this in HT 9. In addition, there are specific building material measures that would have a beneficial impact on indoor air quality.

HT 1 – require use of low-VOC carpets, backing, and cushioning (low cost)

HT 2 – require use of low-VOC paints and glues (low cost)

HT 3 – restrict use of building materials containing formaldehyde (low cost)

HT 4 – require new buildings to install entrance mats that capture particulates (low cost)

HT 14 – remove unnecessary requirements for removal of encased asbestos products (low cost)

a) Current Air Quality Initiative On Point: None

b) Updated Air Quality Initiative: #15– Decrease Toxic Emissions from Building Materials

c) New Implementation Milestone: Introduce and Support Building Code Legislation Requiring the Use of Low Toxic Emissions Materials

WATER
Related Recommendations

1. Combined Sewer Overflows (CSO)

The PlaNYC Water Quality provisions, which incorporate the City's subsequent Sustainable Stormwater Management Plan of 2008, establish a laudable goal of reducing CSOs sufficiently to allow the opening of 90% of our waterways to recreation. Substantial steps towards this goal have already been completed, including stormwater capture facilities and increased green/vegetated surfaces. However, the City's data demonstrate that those steps are falling drastically short. The storage capacity and diversion measures already implemented, plus projected projects, amount to a fraction of the tens of billions of gallons of reduced inputs that must be achieved. Key water quality indicators, harbor-wide dissolved oxygen levels and fecal coliform rates, have both recently moved in the wrong direction (decreased dissolved oxygen and increased fecal coliform). The report attributes the slow progress to the unproven feasibility of alternative strategies, and a lack of funding for implementing more proven strategies. To those, we would add the lack of sufficiently focused metrics with which to set goals and evaluate achievement. Secondly, the current program focuses almost exclusively on public property, while private property in the city accounts for nearly 50% of the total land area responsible for runoff.

A. Data and Coverage

As currently articulated, the CSO plan lacks a data-driven focus on quantifying the needed flow reductions, connecting them to their sources, and evaluating the reductions achieved. In order to develop a comprehensive and effective approach to eliminating CSOs, the PlaNYC policy should be to first quantify the various input elements of the sewer system then calculate the necessary reductions for each sector. The process would begin with an evaluation of overall system capacity, an accounting of sanitary water inputs by sector (residential, commercial and public), followed by an accounting of stormwater impacts by sector. These new data would be used to set targeted, sector-by-sector, sewer use budgets.

a) Current Water Quality Initiative On Point: None

b) Updated Water Quality Initiative: #11– Design a CSO Reduction Plan Driven by Sector-by-Sector Data

c) New Implementation Milestone: Completion of CSO reduction plan for New York City

B. Package of Private Sector Incentives

Once the data and budgets are developed, the City can establish a system of private sector fees, incentives, regulations, and subsidies targeted to achieving the necessary reductions. The incentive system is complementary to the specific pilot programs mentioned in the Built Environment: Water Network and Water Quality sections above. The system should include both the stormwater absorption and retention (the focus of current initiatives) and sanitary water inputs (ignored by current initiatives). There are approximately 1 billion gallons of sanitary water inputs to the sewer system per day in New York City (equal to twice the average daily volume of CSO event discharges).

i) In the stormwater context, this means runoff fees, based on actual impervious area (roofs, pavement, etc.) of a given property. The regulatory-incentive system should offer sufficient credits to drive investment in absorption (vegetation, pervious pavement, etc.) and retention (blue roofs, rain barrels, etc.) technologies, with the fee proceeds being reinvested into subsidies and/or low interest loans for such improvements. Over time, the levy and reinvestment of these fees should be increased incrementally to drive further reductions and innovation.

ii) In the sanitary water context, progressive fees can be established that encourage use reduction (efficiency and conservation) and reuse (gray water). As with the stormwater fees, fees collected for excess sanitary water use should be reinvested into programs stimulating greater reductions and reuse.

a) Current Water Quality Initiative On Point: #9–Provide Incentives for Green Roofs

b) Updated Water Quality Initiative: #9.x–Package of Incentives Aimed at Reducing CSO Inputs from the Private Sector

c) New Implementation Milestone: Introduction of CSO incentive package to City Council

C. Clean Water Action Days

The City should establish "Clean Water Action Days," corresponding to weather driven CSO events, and designed to achieve greater short-term, temporary reductions in peak sanitary water usage. These could involve a combination of heightened public education, including media alerts, imposed flow restrictions on major users, and heightened fees for sanitary water usage above a temporary reduced budget (expressed as a percentage of the normal budget).

a) Current Water Quality Initiative On Point: None

b) Updated Water Quality Initiative: #11.x–Create Clean Water Action Days Program

c) New Implementation Milestone: Implementation of Clean Water Action Days Program

WASTE
Related Recommendations

1. Solid Waste

A. Governance

The production of solid waste, both residential and commercial, is a major source of City-created environmental impacts affecting air, soil, and water quality across a broad geography. Despite the large economic, environmental, and social impacts of municipal solid waste disposition, waste management is not codified as a major area of interest in the PlaNYC model. Neither are there any specific initiatives under other category areas aimed at waste management activities, apart from a general initiative to increase biodiesel blending in the City's truck fleet. The ELC recommends that the new PlaNYC be expanded to include a separate impact category for Waste Management and that cost and impact reduction initiatives based on comprehensive measurement indicators be designed and implemented in the coming years.

a) Current Waste Management Initiative On Point: None

b) Updated Waste Management Initiative: New Scope of Action Category

c) New Implementation Milestone: Inclusion of Waste Management as Major Impact and Initiative Category in all PlaNYC Planning and Reports

B. Waste Reduction

At least 2/3 of New York City's solid waste must be disposed of in landfills located mostly outside New York State. This in turn requires an elaborate network of waste hauling, barging, and landfilling operations stretching as far as Ohio and South Carolina. The cost to the City of this service is approximately $76 per ton for the 10,500 tons per day requiring landfilling (about $300 million per year), and is likely to increase over time due to rising fuel costs.[27] Therefore, initiatives aimed at reducing the stream of solid waste emanating from all sectors would be benefit both the City's budget and the quality of life of its citizens. Therefore, the ELC recommends that a program of solid waste reduction be incorporated into PlaNYC, including such points of action as increases in the recycling rate, implementation of organic waste recycling, MetroCard recycling, variable rate pricing (see Waste Related Energy Reductions in the Energy Recommendations, above), consumer product labeling, and other innovative measures to lessen the City's solid waste footprint.

a) Current Waste Management Initiative On Point: None

b) Updated Waste Management Initiative: #1– Create a Solid Waste Reduction Intergovernmental Task Force for New York City

c) New Implementation Milestone: Commission a comprehensive study of solid waste reduction strategies available to New York City

2. Sewage Waste

An emerging list of wastewater contaminants not being treated by existing treatment facilities is becoming the object of environmental concern around the world.[28] Substances such as personal care product chemicals, pharmaceuticals, nanomaterials, illicit drugs, caffeine, and disinfectant by-products are entering adjacent water bodies and causing metabolic changes in wildlife populations.[29] These contaminants may also enter into biosolids produced by water treatment facilities and then later applied as agricultural amendments.[30] This is an area that requires scrutiny and action by PlaNYC. The first step is to identify and quantify the contaminants being left untreated in the City's wastewater using the latest testing protocols.[31] This study should be followed by a plan of treatment using the latest best practices.[32]

a) Current Water Quality Initiative On Point: #7 – Pilot Promising Best Management Practices (BMP)

b) Updated Waste Management Initiative: #7.x – Commission Testing Study of Emerging Pollutants in Treated Wastewater; Define Treatment Priorities and Options

c) New Implementation Milestone: Publication of emerging pollutants study

Respectfully Submitted
December 22, 2010

Committee on Environmental Law
of the New York City Bar Association

Kathy Robb
CHAIR
Hunton & Williams LLP
200 Park Avenue
New York, NY 10166-0136
Phone: (212) 309-1128
Fax: (212) 309-1100
krobb@hunton.com

Andrew Skroback
SECRETARY

61 Irving Place
Suite 2A
New York, NY 10003
(646) 894-5155
skrobackenvlawcommittee@gmail.com

Adam Cherson

PRINCIPAL AUTHOR

Greencore Environmental Information Services

10 West 66th Street

New York, NY 10023

Phone: (212) 874-7674

adche@xyvy.info

Phillip T. Simpson

PRINCIPAL CONTRIBUTOR

Robinson, Brog, Leinwand, Greene,

Genovese & Gluck, P.C.

875 Third Avenue

New York, NY 10022

Phone: (212) 603-6302

pts@robinsonbrog.com

Christopher Saporita

PRINCIPAL CONTRIBUTOR

Assistant Regional Counsel

Water and General Law Branch

United States Environmental Protection

Agency, Region 2

290 Broadway, 16th Floor

New York, NY 10007

Phone: (212) 637-3203

saporita.chris@epa.gov

Edward Sawchuck, P.E., P.C.
CONTRIBUTOR
381 Park Avenue South, Suite 917
New York, NY 10016
Phone: (212) 682-5990
edwardsawchuck@yahoo.com

Matthew H. Ahrens
Belina Anderson
Ross Brady
Steven Brautigam
Lauren Boccardi
Jean-Philippe Brisson
Jessica L. Campbell
Julie Ann Cilia
Clinton Daggan
Rachel Deming
Arthur Dobelis
Molly McElreth Dunham
Kerry A. Dziubek
Pamela R. Esterman
Victor J. Gallo
Peter P. Garam
Peter J. Gioella, Jr.
Roberta G. Gordon
Edward M. Grauman
Matthew Laudato (student member)
Robin Levine
Kyle A. Lonergan
Stephanie Malkind
Deborah Masucci

Alana D. Mitnick
Timothy J. Mulvihill
Michael G. Murphy
Robert F. Rieske (student member)
Cari Brett Rincker
Kenneth Gary Roberts
Laurie S. Rothenberg
Kate Sinding
Meredith Tinkham (student member)
Niek Veraart

PROTECTING THE GLOBAL COMMMONS IN A PROPRIETARY WORLD

Projects: 1) Presentation at International Marine Debris Conference; 2) Computer Language User Interface (Communications Software)

Entrepreneurial Platform(s): NOAA sponsored International Scientific Conference, Powerpoint; Harvard-Radcliffe 25th Reunion Network

Submitted: 1/11/2011

Background and Description

Protection of the global commons has been my number one subject of interest in the area of international environmental law. It is a major paradox of our international political economy that environmental stewardship is largely dependent on property rights. Since nobody seems to own the atmosphere or the high seas, it seems that these places are free for anyone to pollute. Attempts have been made to establish international norms and standards, but for the most part these are completely voluntary and unenforceable. My interest in marine debris stems from my experience traversing the oceans as a research scuba diver where I assisted a variety of biologists with their projects. Along the way I began to notice that large areas of coral reef seemed to be ghost towns and that beaches everywhere were littered with plastic. During my graduate school days I co-authored a white paper on the subject[33] and have been following the research ever since. The research indicates that marine debris continues to be a problem in the world's oceans and I speculate that the problem of particulate plastic is a contributing factor to the demise of reef ecosystems and fish stocks. Fueled by the growing awareness of this issue, I submitted an abstract to the NOAA conference and was accepted as a presenter. Unfortunately, due to a family illness I was unable to attend.

Effective discussion about the global commons requires the participation of the world's people, communicating with each other intelligibly. For the most part, international environmental communication is conducted in one of the main UN languages, but what of those important minority languages, spoken in so many of the world's environmental hotspots? Since so much of environmental sustainability revolves around knowledge and education, it would seem an imperative that all of those minority peoples be brought into the conversation, and further, that speakers of the main languages also be able to speak with each other without an interpreter. Due to the tools offered by microcomputing and internet communications, what has heretofore been an impossibility now seems do-able: real time, online translation from, and to, any of the world's languages, functionally embedded into social and professional networks. This is the motivational kernel behind the Computer Language User Interface (CLUI). The basic concept is to develop a culturally neutral, meta-language for translation purposes that could be a 'plug-in' for all types of communication software. This would be very, very difficult to put into practice, but ultimately could be a mega, game-changer for an environmentally sustainable globe. With our computer power we can now say that the Tower of Babel is an old-wives tale.

1: A Polluters-Pay System of Liability for the Marine Global Commons[34]

Marine debris, CO2 acidification, eutrophication, and toxic loading, form a suite of pollution threats to the non-territorial marine environment that defies standard notions of legal liability and remedy. Traditional tort-based causes of action are inapposite due to uncertainties of jurisdiction, quantification of damages, and tortfeasor identification. No current international law, treaty-based or customary, creates a cognizable action for environmental damage to the high seas. The unique attributes of pollution in the marine global commons require an entirely new approach to legal policy. The principle of collective-polluters-pay-proportionally makes a firm foundation for a system capable of addressing the scope of the problem. This principle supports strict, no fault liability, and remediation costs (i.e., clean-up costs), assessed proportionally, as the sole measure of damages. Such a system could create the necessary financial deterrent to complement the evolving network of 'soft' global commons law-- the exhortational and aspirational agreements that urge national legislation, regional capacity building, cooperation, and monitoring. This talk will describe the salient aspects of a collective-polluters-pay-proportionally system in the context of marine debris accumulation and the possible promulgation, administration, and enforcement of the system from within the UN Law of the Seas Convention. My goal is to describe one type of reform that could meet the legal and policy challenges presented by marine debris removal from non-territorial waters and could by extension be applied to the other three main forms of pollution threatening the marine global commons. This presentation is intended for the General Law and Policy session under the heading of Legal, Jurisdictional, and Funding Challenges in debris removal.

2: Computer Language User Interface ("CLUI")[35]

OBJECTIVE AND GOALS: 1) to create a computer language user interface for facilitating inter-cultural communication in the information age, 2) to make this language representative of global linguistic diversity, 3) to preserve some remnant of languages that have either already perished from active use or may soon cease to be spoken, 4) to reduce the need for multi-language translation, 5) to keep the language's grammar simple enough to be learned quickly by students, much the same way one might learn basic mathematics, 6) to create an automatic cloud translation platform for conversion of any language into CLUI and vice versa which could be embedded into communication applications (social, professional, news, blog, etc), 7) to create a CLUI Oversight Academy of Standards responsible for expanding vocabulary, alphabet, and grammar as necessitated by experience, 8) to develop optional text to speech add-ons in all languages (CLUI text to language X speech), 9) to expand CLUI vocabularies by means of supervised wikis.

STRATEGIES: 1) simple grammatical rules borrowed from world's easiest languages, 2) eclectic and randomly selected alphabet/pictograms, 3) eclectic and randomly selected vocabulary, 4) use of all known living and dead languages for alphabets, pictographic symbols, punctuation, and vocabularies, 5) allow for use by those who do not want to learn CLUI.

PROCEDURE: The development of CLUI would consist of a series of creation steps: 1) selection of simplest grammatical rules from existing languages

(I am suggesting Mandarin as a starting template based only on my limited knowledge), 2) compilation of languages to be used as a databank for alphabets, vocabularies, and punctuation, 3) selection of initial vocabulary and punctuation list, 4) randomized assignment of CLUI vocabulary to initial vocabulary list, 5) randomized assignment of CLUI alphabetical symbols to CLUI vocabulary, 6) writing would proceed alternatively, left to right and then right to left (boustrophedon), and always from top to bottom.

EXAMPLE: For purposes of this example let's say we are creating a language consisting of only one statement: "I agree with you." Next we compile the list of languages which, for purposes of the example, are Spanish, Chinese, Russian, English, and Greek. Our initial vocabulary list consists of the four words of the statement. The first task is to randomly assign the word from the list of languages that corresponds to the initial vocabulary list. Let's say the assignment happened to occur as follows : I: Chinese (wo), agree: Spanish (acuerdo: we use the infinitive in languages with various verb tenses), with: English (with), and you: Russian (tyh). Now that we know what the sentence will sound like in the new language we can assign the appropriate alphabetical or pictographic symbols. A randomized selection of alphabetic symbols might go like this:

1) since the 'I' comes from a pictographic language, we take the pictograph from that language: 我, and this could become the alphabetic symbol for

that sound everywhere in the language (only if reasonable to do so),

2) for the word acuerdo we simply use the non-pictographic alphabets for each succeeding phoneme or letter; if the randomly drawn language is missing a symbol for that sound or is pictographic, we return that language-alphabet to the unused pile and make another selection; so acuerdo could wind up looking like this:

α (greek) к (russian) w (english) e (spanish) p (russian) d (english) o (spanish): αкwepdo in our dictionary,

3) Now the next time we encounter the 'w' sound we use the English w symbol; so 'with' might become:

w (english), ы (russian), θ (greek) = wыθ,

4) the final word might look something like this:

τ (greek), ы (from prior word)= τы.

The final sentence looks like this:

我
αкwepdo
wыθ
τы

Since we would have a much larger pool of languages and the randomized selection would be done via the elimination of already used languages, the result would be a fairly evenly distributed combination of vocabulary from all of the languages. The language symbols would be limited to the number of phonemes required by the vocabulary and may not wind up including all of the languages in the pool since there would probably be fewer distinct phonemes than there are languages.

The result would be a language that draws its alphabet and vocabulary from all the human languages and thus minimizes translation confusion as well as choice of language bias. Furthermore, the existence of a CLUI would facilitate translation of texts from all the world's languages into any other of the world's languages simply by knowing one language besides your own: originator prepares translation from Language A into CLUI while recipient need then only translate from CLUI into Language B.

EMERGENCY ASSISTANCE FOLLOWING ENVIRONMENTAL DISASTERS

Project: Humanitarian Air Drop

Entrepreneurial Platform(s): Innocentive Challenge; Huddle; Google Sketchup and other CAD

Submitted: 3/2/2011

Background

The challenge asked for an engineered solution allowing for large, safe, and widely dispersed emergency supply drops from B-130 aircraft to populations far below. This project was a collaborative effort with the aerospace engineer Ryuhei Ishikawa. We had to work within certain aircraft and cargo parameters. We produced five variations around the concept of the tubachute (which was jointly developed). The tubachute is a self-contained parachute enclosing individually packaged supplies whose release is triggered open by a small built-in device at a pre-set height above the ground.

The particular variation I show here (heavy-duty rollers) was mainly my concept. The computer assisted drawings were all prepared by my collaborator.

The Challenge

The Challenge is to modify the delivery system or come up with a new system that can quickly get these food and water packages out of the aircraft at the drop point and have them scatter the contents on the ground. Ideally, only the food and water packages would hit the ground which has been designed to not cause harm to humans below. If anything else falls to the ground, it should be light enough not to cause damage to humans.

Any proposed solution should address the following Technical Requirements:

1. The system must be able to release 22,400 lbs. for the C-130 (56,000 lbs. for the C-17), with meal packages ranging from 0.12 to 2.25 lbs. and corresponding volumes of 3 to 180 cubic inches.

2. The whole load (or a partial load) should be able to be released at the drop point in 10 seconds or less. Note: Currently, the whole load is released at multiple drop point limited by the number of containers. It would be desirable if the system was flexible enough such that a load could be split up into groups and dropped at different drop points. (e.g.

drop 5 containers at point 1, 4 containers at point 2 and 7 containers at point 3)

3. Once released, the food and water items should scatter and fall independently of each other and any other material.

4. Any non-food item that is released by the aircraft during the drop must be light and/or small enough to not be a falling hazard to humans on the ground. It is preferable if nothing but the food items actually leaves the aircraft.

5. The system must be compatible with current C-130E/H/J and C-17 aircraft. It cannot require changes/alterations to the airframe and must be considered safe for the aircraft and crew members. Note: The current roller system may be removed/stowed and new equipment can be placed inside the aircraft for deployment. Alternatively, you can modify the roller system. All equipment should be modular and removable.

6. The airdrop altitude can be no lower than 2,000 ft. AGL (above ground level) and no higher than 35,000 ft. MSL (mean sea level).

7. The system should be able to handle Inflight g-loading at 2G vertical, 3G forward, 1,5G aft & lateral.

8. The proposed system must be able to be preloaded in a separate storage area and able to load onto the aircraft in a matter of hours using a standard loader, forklift or palette mover.

9. The proposed system should offer the Seeker client "freedom to practice" and be available for licensing. There should be no third party patent art preventing the use of specific equipment and materials for their commercial application.

The Solution

HUMANITARIAN AIR DROP

Innocentive Challenge ID: 9932741

Introduction

We present a delivery system capable of safely and accurately scattering food and water packages from aviation altitudes anytime and anywhere throughout the world. Our custom-designed system resolves the technical challenges by using ultra-strong and lightweight packaging materials, a gravity mediated drop system and an engineered scatter mechanism. Together, these elements create a low-cost system that will allow rapid loading, multiple drop points from any altitude, widespread scattering, failsafe reliability, no extraneous falling debris, and safety for system operators and relief recipients. In order to illustrate the operation of this system within the context of the challenge's technical requirements, we present a simulated relief mission annotated with specifications and drawings.

Mission

To load on to an unaltered C-130 aircraft, within several hours, using forklifts and a standard loader, 22,400 lbs of food and water supplies ranging in size from 3 to 180 cubic inches and weighing between 0.12 and 2.25 lbs, and ready for deployment as follows: 1) 7,467 lbs of supplies dropped from an altitude of 2,000 feet above ground level (agl) so as to scatter around target A, located at sea level; 2) 7,467 lbs of supplies dropped from an altitude of 20,000 feet agl so as to scatter around target B, located at 1,000 feet agl; 3) 7,467 lbs of supplies dropped from an altitude of 35,000 feet agl so as to scatter around target B, located at 10,000 feet agl.

Tubachute

The tubachute is an engineered sack having dimensions of 4 feet in length and 2.5 feet in diameter. The tubachute container is entirely made from standard 500 Denier Cordura Nylon (weight 6.5oz./sq). The sack consists of a wrap-around design as shown in **Image A**. The container is created as the lower shell assembly is rolled in on itself as shown in the illustration, creating a triple-stitched tube enclosed by two circular pieces of material at each end. As shown in the illustration, one side of the container is pierced by a cut-out opening of 1' x 1 2/3'. This opening is covered over by the upper shell assembly as it wraps around the main body of the container. The inside edges of the upper (tapered) shell assembly are lined with the hook side of a 1.5 inch wide, hook-and-fastener tape[36] which is triple-stitched on to the shell assembly. The 1.5 inch fastener side of the tape is stitched to the exterior of the lower shell assembly such that it will fasten with the upper shell as it is rolled on to the surface of the container. The hook-and-fastener system is designed to be strong enough to hold the upper assembly attached to the surface of the contained together yet pliable enough to be ripped open by the brake parachute's opening force. The required test strength of the hook-and-fastener system is estimated to be 200 lbs. as compared to the brake parachute's opening force of 320 pounds.

At the end of the tapered side of the shell assembly is small plastic housing for a 2 foot diameter parachute and an automatic activation device (AAD), **Image B (shown while opening).** The parachute is constructed of clear nylon and weighs about 5 pounds (2.3kg). The AAD can function in either one of two modes, altitude or timer. In timer mode, the device will release the parachute after a user-defined time interval. In altitude mode the parachute release will occur at the user-defined altitude (however only when the altitude is reached after a descent). When the parachute is released a jolting force of 320 lbs. causes the hook-and-fastener tape to come undone, in turn causing the upper shell to peel off the container as shown in **Image C**. As the shell unfurls and the parachute inflates, the cut-out opening is revealed and supplies begin to fall freely. The force of the parachute causes the container to fold outward, as shown in **Image A (position 7B)**, thereby expelling the remaining contents. Since the empty container weighs more than the parachute, the empty container floats to the ground somewhere near the target. The empty container shell may be used on the ground as a shelter, blanket, or tarp. The brake parachute material is usable as a solar powered water purification system if so desired.

Pre-Loading

The tubachute is packed with relief supplies through an opening at the top of the container. The supplies are poured in at random until the net weight of container reaches 550 pounds or fraction thereof according to the drop plan, **Image D**. Due to the random sorting of the supplies within the containers and the flexibility of the containers themselves, they are directly stackable to two levels and offset stackable to three levels (pyramid shape with each level consisting of one less container, **Image E**). For this mission, a total of 39, 550 pound containers, and three, 317 pound containers are pre-packed. The 'V' side is then latched closed and the container is ready for loading. Each AAD is set according to the mission's drop plan (this last step may be done at any time prior to cargo loading). For this mission we prepare three sets of 14 containers, using the AADs in altitude mode. Each set consists of 13@550 pounds and 1@317. The 14 AADs for the first set (Drop A) are set to open at 750 feet above sea level, a point 750 feet above ground level at that spot.[37] The 14 AADs for the second set (Drop B) are set to open at 1,750 feet above sea level, a point 750 feet above ground level there. The 14 AADs for the third set (Drop C) are set to open at 10,750 feet, once again a point 750 feet above ground level there. Each container is tagged, labeled, and numbered with drop-specific information.

Cargo Bay Preparation

The C-130 cargo bay is prepared as follows: 1) C-130 roller units are removed from cargo bay area (but not from the rear plank), 2) heavy duty roller conveyor modules, **Image F**, are installed on to the floor of the cargo area; the modules are installed three across and nine deep with about 1.5' of spacing between each column of rollers. In order to allow forklift loading of the containers inside the cargo hold, the modules are installed, loaded, and secured by webbing one group of three at a time from fore to aft. The roller modules are labeled 1 to 9 from fore to aft and A to C from port to starboard.

Loading

The containers may be moved by forklift as shown in **Image G**. These containers may be stacked two high on to a standard loader for loading on to the C-130. The containers are loaded into the cargo area using a forklift. The loading procedure consists of installing one set of three rollers, **Image H**, loading containers on to these rollers using the forklift so that the containers are parallel with the rollers, **Image E**, and then restraining these containers with heavy webbing to the aircraft's central and lateral restraint systems, all before proceeding to install the next set of rollers. As the containers are loaded the loadmaster confirms the AAD settings are accurate for various drop points. The first group of 14 containers (Drop C) are loaded as follows: on rollers 1A and 1B, one container each. Roller 1C is unoccupied. On rollers 2A to 2C, 6 containers in a pyramidal configuration (3 containers directly on the rollers, 2 above and between those, and 1 more above and between those). Rollers 3A to 3C are loaded in the same way as 2A to 2C . Webbing is rigged so as to allow cutting and release when loadmaster is clear. The same process is followed for the Drop B and Drop A containers. When the loading is complete, the Drop A containers will be closest to the rear of the aircraft and all three groupings will be secure and rigged for individual release at the appropriate moment.

In-Flight Preparation

Unless there is a change in mission targets, the AADs have already been set on the ground and double-checked upon loading so that no further attention to them is required. In case of emergency, they may be reset in-flight to the extent that the AADs are accessible and not underneath other containers. The loadmaster prepares to cut the restraining webbing prior to each drop.

Drop 1

At the drop point, the rear ramp is opened, the plane assumes a 7 degree skyward angle, and the restraining webbing is cut on the group of containers closest to the ramp. The containers roll swiftly off the conveyor and on to the ramp where they fall out of the plane. Once the designated containers are gone, the ramp is closed. The containers fall until releasing the brake parachutes, whereupon their contents are released for a scattered free-fall, **Image F**.

Drop 2

The process repeats for the next group of containers as described for the first drop.

Drop 3

The process repeats for the next group of containers as described for the first drop.

Scattering of Supplies

For each drop, the containers fall freely until the supplies are released at the pre-determined altitude (normally this will be 750 feet agl at the target location). At this point the AAD releases the brake parachute on each container, **Image C**. This braking action forces the container open and allow the supplies to fall out, **Image I**. It is estimated that the supplies from each drop will scatter freely to an area about 1 mile (1.5 km) long by about 328 feet (100 m) wide[38]. The empty containers, supported by their brake parachutes, will also fall near this area. The containers are designed for use as shelters and tarps in the relief area. A small cash reward may be offered for return of the AADs, if feasible.

Rationale

1. The system must be able to release 22,400 lbs. for the C-130 (56,000 lbs. for the C-17), with meal packages ranging from 0.12 to 2.25 lbs. and corresponding volumes of 3 to 180 cubic inches.

Each tubachute container is designed to hold 550 lbs in packages ranging in size from 3 to 180 cubic inches and weighing between 0.12 and 2.25 lbs. *The total amount of supplies released is limited only by the cargo capacity of the aircraft making the drop. As compared to the TRIADS system, this system produces a more accurate drop to the target since the release of individual relief packages occurs at roughly 750 feet[39] over the target no matter the drop altitude from the C-130.*

2. The whole load (or a partial load) should be able to be released at the drop point in 10 seconds or less. Note: Currently, the whole load is released at multiple drop point limited by the number of containers. It would be desirable if the system was flexible enough such that a load could be split up into groups and dropped at different drop points (e.g. drop 5 containers at point 1, 4 containers at point 2 and 7 containers at point 3).

The roller conveyor system is configurable to permit anywhere from 1 (full load of 41 containers) to 27 (1 container) drops, each consisting of any number of containers (subject only to cargo capacity and logistical limits, Image J (shows maximum possible number of containers). This release system will assure a rapid (less than 10 seconds) and accurate release of supplies for any one of multiple targets on any given mission. As compared to the TRIADS system, this system produces greater mission flexibility since any number of containers may be dropped at any number of targets subject only to capacity and logistical limits .

3. Once released, the food and water items should scatter and fall independently of each other and any other material.

The tubachute is engineered to carry the supplies from the aircraft to a specified altitude above the drop point. Once the tubachute brake is triggered, the container unravels, releasing the supplies for a randomly scattered free-fall around the target. The supplies will fall independently of other material. The parachuted container will fall separately from the food and water items.

4. Any non-food item that is released by the aircraft during the drop must be light and/or small enough to not be a falling hazard to humans on the ground. It is preferable if nothing but the food items actually leaves the aircraft.

The tubachute containers will float gently down to the ground supported by their brake parachutes. These containers are designed for use as shelters or tarps on the ground while the brake parachutes may be used as solar water disinfection systems. All portions of the drop have a rescue value and therefore nothing falls to the ground that is not usable by the recipients on the ground.

5. The system must be compatible with current C-130E/H/J and C-17 aircraft. It cannot require changes/alterations to the airframe and must be considered safe for the aircraft and crew members. **Note:** The current roller system may be removed/stowed and new equipment can be placed inside the aircraft for deployment. Alternatively, you can modify the roller system. All equipment should be modular and removable.

The drop logistics described above are designed for deployment from a C-130 or C-17 aircraft, without alterations to the mainframe. The heavy duty roller conveyor units are modular and removable. They can be stacked and moved by pallet. The individual rollers are each of 2-1/2" diameter x 11 gauge. They are each individually replaceable. The roller centers are 4" apart. The load capacity of the roller system is as follows: given supports spaced at 5 foot intervals, the maximum uniformly distributed load for each section is 5,200 lbs. The maximum load per roller is 650 lbs.[40]

6. The airdrop altitude can be no lower than 2,000 ft. AGL (above ground level) and no higher than 35,000 ft. MSL (mean sea level).

The tubachute trigger mechanism is designed to release supplies at a defined altitude above the target (for a broadly scattered dispersion, 750 agl feet is suggested[41]). This mechanism is pre-set on the ground depending on the altitude of the drop and may be adjusted in-flight if necessary and if the trigger mechanism is accessible. The system can function for a drop from any altitude from 2,000 to 35,000 feet.

7. The system should be able to handle Inflight g-loading at 2G vertical, 3G forward, 1,5G aft & lateral.

The tubachute containers are 4 feet x 2.5 feet and have a maximum net weight of 550 lbs each. They will be strapped to the aircraft's restraint systems in much the same way as the TRIADS are restrained. The heavy duty roller conveyor is fixed to the fuselage in much the same way as the C-130's removable roller system. Given proper restraint, the containers and the rollers can sustain the required loads. According to the Challenge requirements, solutions are not expected to detail webbing design.

8. The proposed system must be able to be preloaded in a separate storage area and able to load onto the aircraft in a matter of hours using a standard loader, forklift or palette mover.

The heavy duty roller conveyor units are modular and removable. They can be stacked and moved by pallet. The tubachute containers are essentially open sacks and are loaded through an opening at the top of the container. Then the sack is fastened and hoisted on to a pallet. Four containers may be loaded on to a single pallet. These pallets may be shrink-wrapped for additional security, but are not stackable. The pallets may be transported via any traditional means to the aircraft loading area. At the loading area, the containers are hoisted off the pallets and then loaded on to the roller conveyors by forklift (or optionally by winch). The containers are then secured by restraint webbing.

9. The proposed system should offer the Seeker client "freedom to practice" and be available for licensing. There should be no third party patent art preventing the use of specific equipment and materials for their commercial application.

The tubachute technology and the drop deployment system have both been designed by the Solvers specifically for this challenge and are available for licensing or assignment. There is no third party patent art preventing the use of the tubachute technology or drop deployment system and the Seeker is free to implement the technology and the system. The materials being used for the tubachutes and the drop deployment system are commercially available without the need for special licensing or permission. Other required equipment is standard loading and rigging machinery.

Equipment and Hardware Costs (net of fuel and labor)

Delivery Equipment

Tubachute

(1 per 550 lbs of supply cargo;
41(or 42) for 22,400 lbs)
31.4ft^2 500 Denier Cordura Nylon
\$0.15/ft^2 = \$ 4.71
1 AAD \$8.00 = \$ 8.00
\$12.71 X 41 = \$521.11

Cord As Needed Cost unknown

Webbing As Needed Cost unknown

Tape As Needed Cost unknown

Delivery System Total \$521.11 (\$0.023/lb MRE/HDR)

Relief Supplies

MREs and HDRs 22,400 lbs
Cost unknown

Shelters and Tarps 1 per Tubachute;
41(or 42) per full load Free

Solar Disinfection System 1 per Tubachute;
41(or 42) per full load Free

Capital Equipment

Heavy Duty Roller Conveyor

27 Sections @ 48"x33-1/4OAW[42]

$ 5,062.50

Supports and hardware

$ 2,000.00

$ 7,062.50

Pallets (1 per 4 Tubachutes) Existing Equipment

No additional cost

Forklift Existing Equipment

No additional cost

Standard Loader Existing Equipment

No additional cost

C-130 Aircraft Existing Equipment

No additional cost

Project Additional Total $ 7,062.50

Assuming 50 missions per year for 10 years ($0.0063/lb MRE/HDR)

TOTAL COST PER POUND OF MRE/HDR[43]

($0.0293/lb MRE/HDR)

APPENDIX OF CALCULATIONS

Tubachute Braking Calculations

The braking force of the parachute is calculated to be 150 kg = 320 lbs.

This is the approximate force exerted opposite the fall by a 2 foot parachute on an object falling at 492 feet per second which is the terminal velocity of the tubachute. The tubachute's construction is designed to unravel at a force of 250 lbs.

Empty Tubachute Landing Calculations

Using $F_D = 1/2\ \varrho u^2 C_D A$ -----> $u = (2\ F_D / (\varrho\ C_D\ A))^{1/2}$

where

F_D is the force of gravity, (weight of empty tubachute + parachute) x 9.8 m/sec^2

ϱ is the mass density of the fluid, ($\approx$ 1 kg/m3)

u is the velocity of the object relative to the fluid, (m/sec)

A is the reference area, (m_2) (.61m diameter parachute)

C_D is the drag coefficient ($\approx$ 1)

The landing speed may be calculated. The speed of the empty tubachute landing is not expected to exceed 9.7 m/sec = 31.824 f/sec.

Supply Scatter Calculation

The area of scattering will be decided in early stages of each drop by how quickly the containers will get freed up from the blanket and start its free falling. If we assume that it takes 10 seconds to drag the 14 containers out from the plane, there will be a difference of ten seconds from the first container to the last. If the pane is traveling at about 492 feet/sec, the scattering distance will be about 1 mile. Until the AAD releases the brake chute, the containers are falling freely, straight down to the ground, in the order they were let free of the blanket and perhaps affected by prevailing winds. Once the supplies are released, the only scattering force will be prevailing winds, if any. It may take few seconds to open the container and complete the release of all the supplies, but the scattering effect from 750 feet agl to the ground will not be very large. The width of the scatter will be determined only by how the supply packages fly around in the air from 750 feet agl. A sage assumption might be to say that the lighter materials may cover a width of about 328 feet. The estimated total scatter area in the absence of enlargement by wind is about 39 acres.

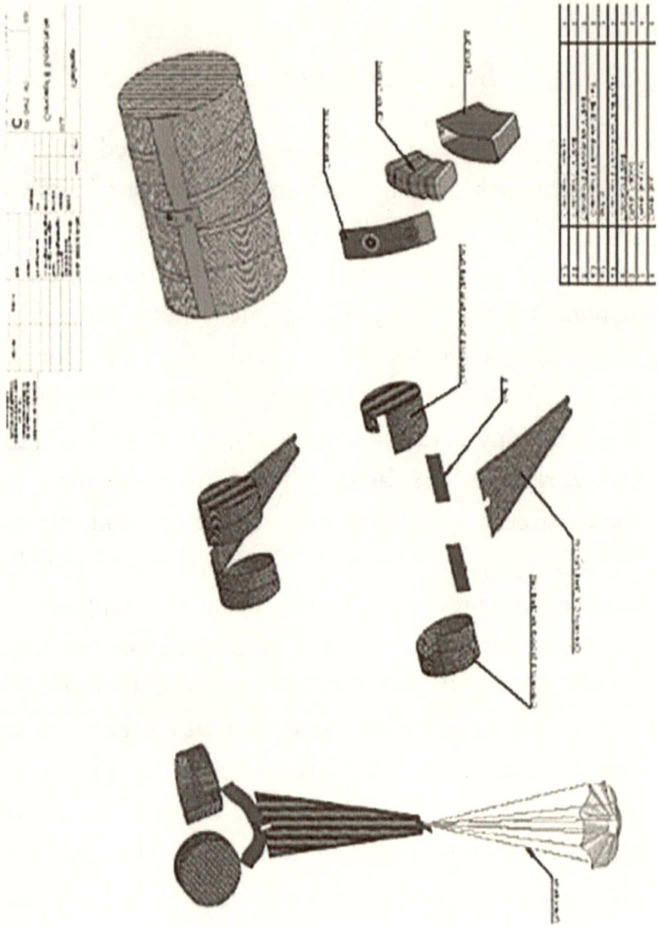

Fig. A: hi-res color image:
http://image.xyvy.info/image035hires.jpg

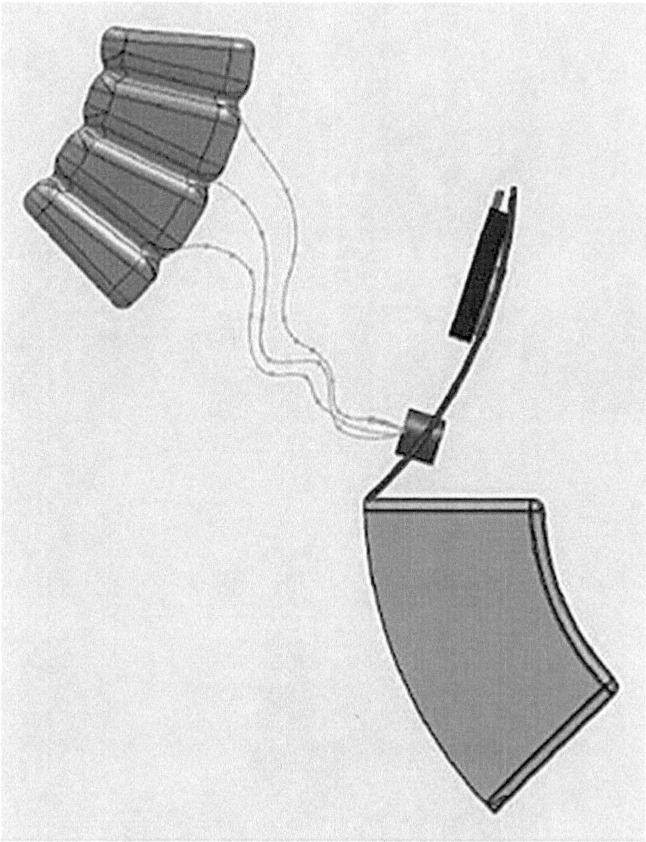

Fig. B: hi-res color image:
http://image.xyvy.info/image036hires.jpg

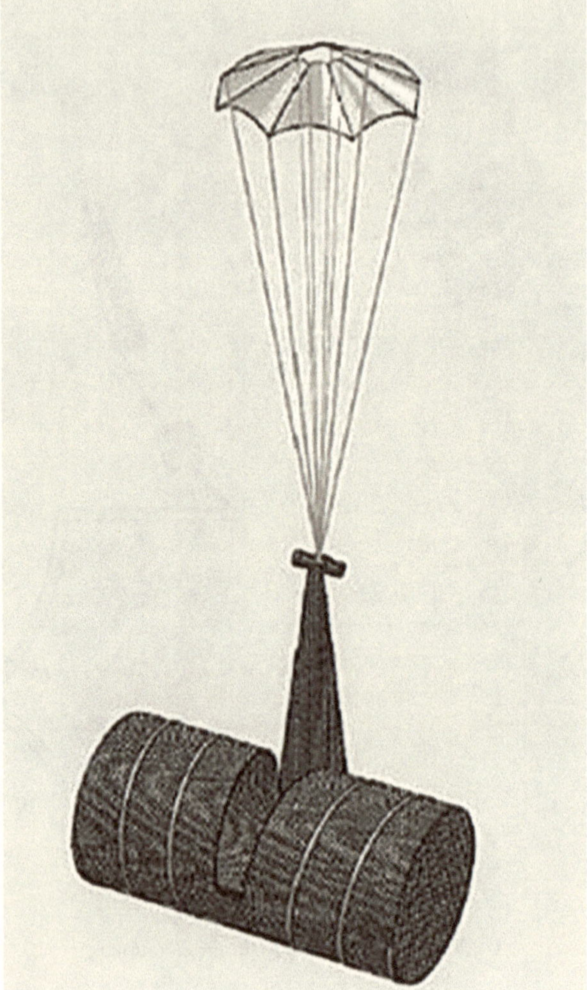

Fig. C: hi-res color image:
http://image.xyvy.info/image037hires.jpg

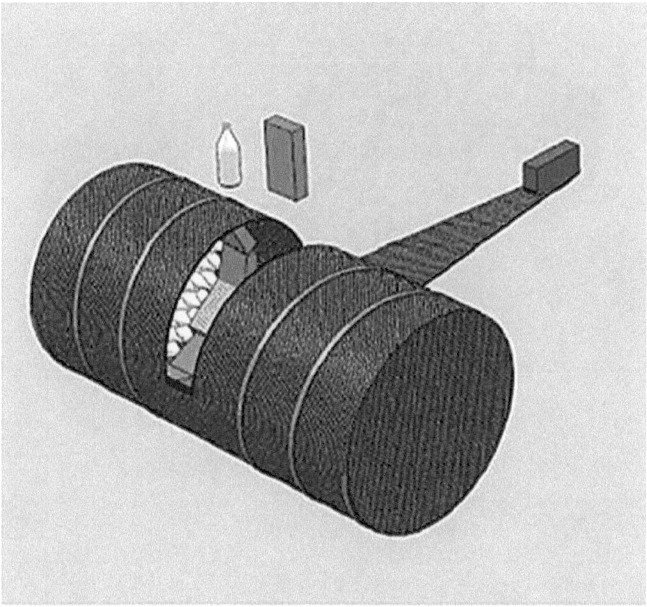

Fig. D: hi-res color image:
http://image.xyvy.info/image038hires.jpg

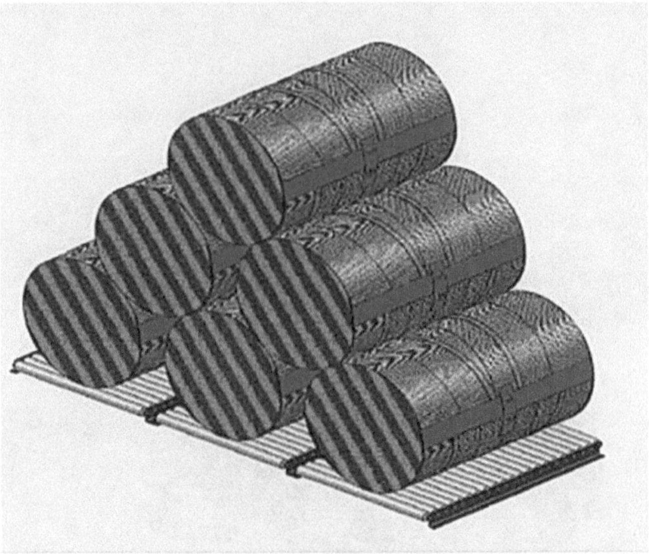

Fig. E: hi-res color image:
http://image.xyvy.info/image039hires.jpg

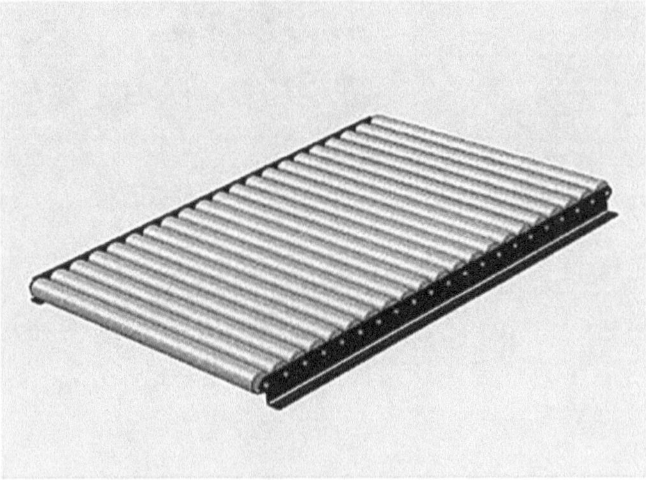

Fig. F: hi-res color image:
http://image.xyvy.info/image040hires.jpg

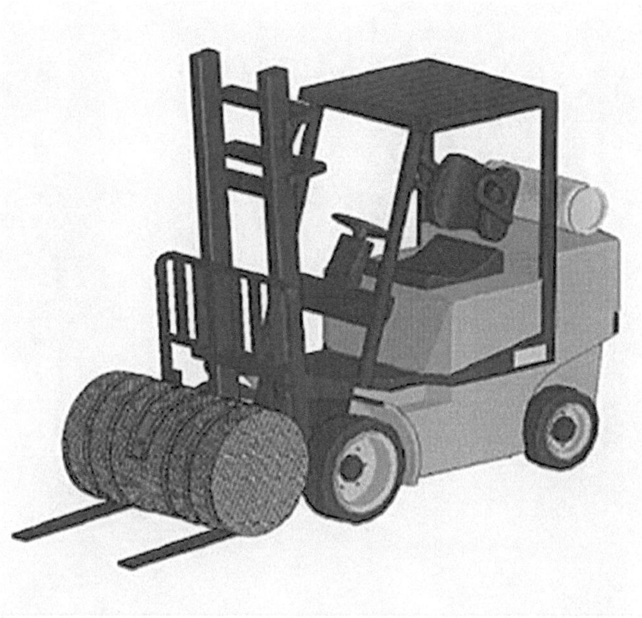

Fig. G: hi-res color image:
http://image.xyvy.info/image041hires.jpg

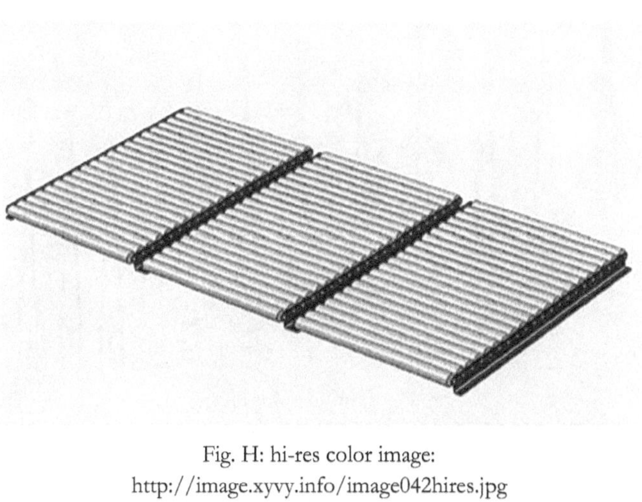

Fig. H: hi-res color image:
http://image.xyvy.info/image042hires.jpg

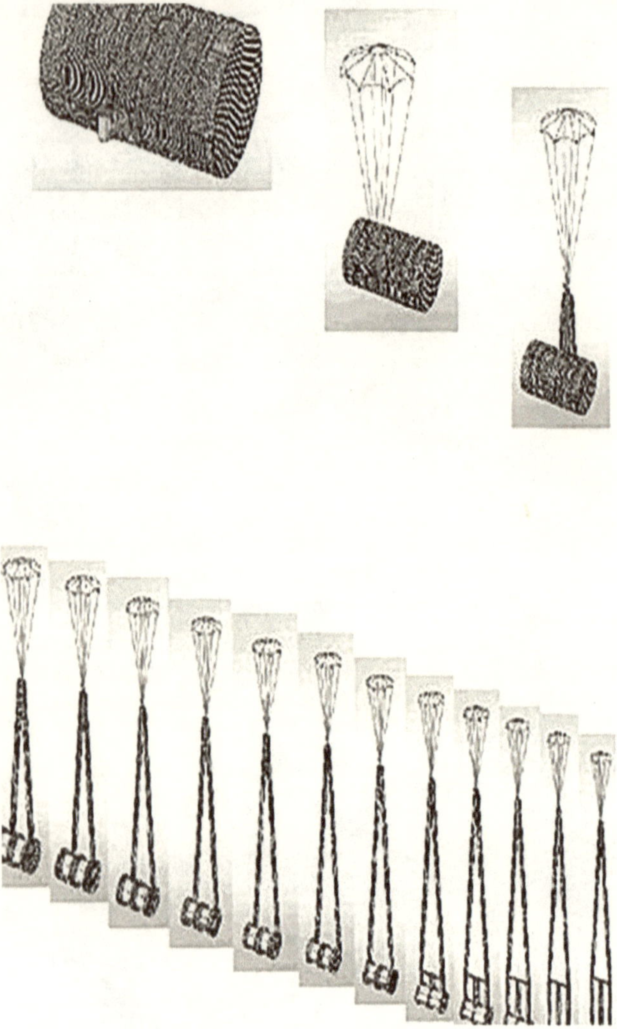

Fig. I: hi-res color image:
http://image.xyvy.info/image043hires.jpg

FIG. J: hi-res color image:
http://image.xyvy.info/image044hires.jpg

USING BIG DATA TO DEVELOP HUMAN POTENTIAL

Project: Intellectual Energy Index (IEI)

Entrepreneurial Platform(s): The Economist/ Innocentive Challenge; Microsoft Excel,

Submitted: 5/6/2011

Background

The challenge was to come up with a metric or index that would capture the enabling of human potential. Statistical indices based on big data metrics are the bread and butter of environmental sustainability so I leaped at the task. I developed my IEI based on a combination of well-established socioeconomic metrics and a few of my own invention. The result is a statistically sound approach to making this measurement of intellectual energy across groups, societies, and nations. Of particular practical interest is the use of the system as a policy making strategy. As shown in the example, a careful analysis of the index sub-components can illuminate focus areas for policy action.

The Challenge

In September 2011, The Economist will be hosting a conference on the theme of Human Potential part of their Ideas Economy conference series. Innocentive and The Economist are teaming up to run a Challenge as a means of recognizing and drawing attention to promising ideas that embody the conference's topics...This Challenge touches upon a very interesting theme emerging from the conference – metrics. Societal, environmental, governmental and economic metrics and indices have long been known to be tremendously useful tools for tracking the progress of humankind. For example, Bhutan's 'Gross National Happiness' index has helped that country's government better manage its population's contentment and make changes for those parts of the country that were lagging. Similarly, there's the commission on the measurement of economic performance and social progress that focuses on quantifying the output of the economy and society of France. And finally a third example is the OECD's quality of life index which tries to quantify how many of the world's economies are growing and evolving based on the governance and policies they enact.

The objective of this Challenge is for you to come up with your own metric or index that will capture an important element of society. The metric or index should be relevant to the conference's main theme of enabling human potential; defined as: how successfully individuals, organizations, and societies are able to unleash intellectual energy and capitalize on it for social and economic progress. While you may not be able to start quantifying your metric or index yet, you should be able to reasonably explain where you would be able to locate the data that you need both now and in the future. You can assume that the creation of some reasonable data collection infrastructure would be possible, though that is beyond the scope of the Challenge. Even though a metric or index could be used to quantify local trends of human potential, it's more interesting to the Economist to learn about metrics or indices that measure trends at least at the country or regional level, if not at the global level.

The Solution

INTELLECTUAL ENERGY INDEX (IEI)[44]

Innocentive Challenge ID: 9932801

This challenge asks us to design a metric or index for measuring conditions favoring the deployment and application of human intellectual energy. We are challenged to build a predictive model, one that focuses on potential, on the 'unleashing of intellectual energy' into the future. Since there is not, to my knowledge, a direct metric for 'intellectual energy', nor could there ever be a single proxy variable for this quality, I have developed a multivariate index, the 'Intellectual Energy Index' (IEI), capable of quantifying this elusive property. This solution includes a description of results and methods as well as a hypothetical illustration of policy analysis using these results.

Executive Summary

A seven factor IEI was created using rigorous statistical testing (described below). *The IEI measures a test group's potential to sustain or improve upon its current socioeconomic performance in the short, medium, and long term as a function of intellectual energy potential.* A validation study conducted on a sample of 50 nations representing about 75% of the world's population, shows that the IEI has strong predictive power in explaining the rate of change of GDP growth (per capita) projected to the year 2016 (<GDP-grpc; see Table 1). The <GDP variable consists of the slope of the line created by International Monetary Fund GDP projections and measures how fast this GDP growth is changing. I chose the variable <GDP-grpc as the initial IEI validator since it seems reasonable to view changes in the rate of GDP growth as an effect of unleashed intellectual energy and, besides, it is the only metric of any kind for which I could find sufficient data with which to test current IEI results. We must remember though that 'intellectual energy' is not the same socioeconomic property as GDP growth: in fact my results shows there can be

very large disparities in performance between these two measurements within one nation. Validation of the IEI with respect to current HDI (Human Development Index) was also convincing: adjusted R^2=.79161, p=.0000 and could be conducted for HDI growth as well, given sufficient time series data. IEI validation vis-a-vis cultural performance will require the completion or expansion of metrics such as UNESCO's Cultural Index. Validation using satisfaction or happiness indices such as the Happy Planet Index or the Gallup World Poll is not advisable since these qualities are too subjective and culturally-defined to allow for cross country comparison.

Regression (x to <GDP-grpc)	*# of Variables*	*R^2*	*Significance*
Intellectual Energy Index (A)	7[43]	.8518 (Adjusted)[44]	p=.0000 <.05
Intellectual Energy Index (B)	6	.8534 (Adjusted)[45]	p=.0000 <.05
Human Development Index	4	.7875 (Adjusted)[46]	p=.0000 <.05
2010 GNI-pc	1	.6596	p=.0000 <.05
Index of Economic Freedom	10	.5426 (Adjusted)[47]	p=.0000 <.05
Democracy Index	5	.5237 (Adjusted)[48]	p=.0000 <.05

Table 1: Validation of IEI and comparison with regressions using several other indices and metrics

IEI Description and Discussion of Index Variables

From the many statistical variables capable, at least in theory, of measuring aspects of intellectual energy, I made an initial broad selection based on several criteria: 1) opting for metrics for which ample and current data exist openly to the public, 2) avoiding expenditure-type statistics (eg. metrics such as ‘percent of national budget spent on health care or education’); I am not persuaded that expenditure is always a reliable indicator of achievement, and 3) opting to incorporate existing multi-component indices instead of single factor statistics in order to capture greater system complexity with the smallest number of variables. The initially selected variables were tested individually for bivariate correlational strength, significance levels, assumptions,[45] and theoretical soundness and then combined into the most parsimonious explanatory model using comparative multivariate regression. The result is an index-model which brings together various traditional socioeconomic statistics such as life expectancy, education (both included in HDI variable), and freedom (GPI variable) along with several new statistics, designed by the Solver, incorporating additional factors such as food and energy security (including population and migration impacts), and globality (explained below). Together these variables measure the extent to which members of any study group have the freedom, motivation, and resources to innovate and the extent to which innovations are adopted.

Factor	Dimension	Variable (Statistic or Index)	Source
Food Security	Fertile Soil	Soil Sufficiency (S)	Created by Solver
Energy Security	Energy Supply and Demand	Net Energy (S)	Created by Solver
Prior Development	Health, Education, Income	HDI (I)	UNDP
Incentive	Return on Individual Effort	GINI (S)"	CIA Factbook
Globality	Inclusive Fitness	Genetic Diversity (S)	Created by Solver
Ecology	Environmental Performance	EPI (I)	CIESIN/CELP
Political Will	Peace and Freedom	GPI (I)	Economist Intel Unit

Table 2: IEI Factors, Dimensions, and Variables

Food Security: Soil Sufficiency (Statistic)

Fertile Soil is a statistic created by the Solver for this challenge. This variable reveals amount of fertile soil per capita within the territory, adjusted for the natural population growth and the net migration rates. Natural population growth is defined as the number of live births minus the number of deaths during the year. Net migration is the difference between immigration into and emigration from the territory during the year. This statistic, which may also be considered as a proxy for water availability, is justified for the IEI by reasoning that says soil fertility provides a secure foundation with which to nourish a population, thereby allowing time for intellectual pursuits. The impact horizon for this variable is constant over time. Data on forest and arable land areas, population growth, and net migration are widely available, frequently updated, and comprehensive. The population and growth data used to prepare this solution are drawn from the United Nations Human Development Report web site; the migration data is from the CIA Factbook, and the forest and arable land data are from the UN Food and Agriculture Organization.

Energy Security: Net Energy (Statistic)

Net Energy is a variable created by the Solver that calculates the difference between total energy production per capita and total energy consumption per capita, adjusted for the natural population growth and the net migration rates. This variable is a reasonable representation of the group's energy security and is justified for the IEI by reasoning that says intellectually driven activity usually requires an ample energy supply to flourish, especially if climate change predictions requiring large scale adaptations come to pass. The impact horizon for this variable is constant. Data on energy production and consumption are widely available, frequently updated, and comprehensive. The raw data used to prepare this variable are drawn from online materials maintained by the United States Department of Energy's International Energy Agency.

Prior Development: Human Development (Index)

The Human Development Index is prepared by the United Nations Development Programme and averages socioeconomic achievements in a country using four statistics: life expectancy at birth, mean years of schooling, expected years of schooling, and gross national income per capita. The HDI provides a snapshot of prior development within the group at the moment of measurement, delivering current-state information three obvious intellectual energy catalysts: health, educational, and communal wealth. These statistics, in particular health and wealth results, also reflect the extent to which innovations tend to be adopted and promulgated within this society. Inclusion of these statistics is justified for the IEI by reasoning that says that access to knowledge and information (schooling), good health (life expectancy), and income (gni-pc) all stimulate the utilization and application of intellectual energy. The impact horizon for this variable is the short to medium term. The HDI data are publicly available, cover most of the world, and are regularly updated. The HDI data used to prepare this solution are drawn from the United Nations Human Development Report web site.

Incentive: GINI Coeffecient (Statistic)

Distributional equity metrics assess the evenness of wealth distribution. Of the many statistics available to measure this quality one of the simplest to understand and use is the Gini-coefficient. This statistic tells how far evenly wealth is distributed to families within the group. A value of 0 means completely equal distribution and of 100 means complete concentration of wealth in the hands of one family. This variable expresses the degree to which group economic rewards are shared among families and is justified for the IEI by reasoning that says distribution of wealth creates an incentive for individual intellectual effort. The impact horizon for this variable is the short to medium term. Gini data are widely available, cover most of the world, but tend to be less regularly updated than other economic statistics (still, the Gini offers the most complete available set of data covering wealth distribution). The Gini data used to prepare this solution are drawn from the United Nations Human Development Report web site. Depending on the user's theoretical affinities, this variable may be omitted in favor of the six variable IEI.

Globality: Genetic Diversity (Statistic)

Genetic diversity is a statistic created by the Solver for this challenge. The statistic is a proxy for actual genetic diversity within the group. The variable is calculated using the well known Shannon diversity formula as applied to two particular human genes, mitochondrial DNA and Y-DNA (currently only Y-DNA data has been compiled). This statistic is justified for the IEI by reasoning that says genetic diversity increases the intellectual fitness of the group by providing greater variability for selection. The impact horizon for this variable is long term. This data used to prepare this solution have been collated by the Solver from the genetic ancestry research literature, a literature that is frequently updated, expanded, and widely published in several prominent journals.

Ecology: Environmental Performance (Index)

The Environmental Performance Index is co-authored by the Center for International Earth Science Information Network at Columbia University and the Yale Center for Environmental Law & Policy. The index ranks 163 countries on 25 performance indicators tracked across ten policy categories covering both environmental public health and ecosystem vitality. Environmental performance data provides an insight into the group's rate of depletion of natural capital resources and is justified for the IEI by reasoning that says natural capital is an exhaustible and a necessary catalyst of intellectual energy. The impact horizon for this variable is long term. The environmental performance data utilized by the EPI are widely available and comprehensive. The index is updated regularly and available publicly.

Political Will: Global Peace (Index)

The GPI, drawn from data collected by the Economist Intelligence Unit and measuring the relative peacefulness of nations, incorporates 23 indicators such as number of wars fought, number of heavy weapons, number of homicides, likelihood of violent crime, and number of jailed persons to arrive at an overall score. The index ranks 149 countries, is updated annually, and is open-use. The GPI is justified for the IEI by reasoning that says greater safety and security for individuals within the group means more time and resources available for intellectual pursuits. The impact horizon for this variable is short to medium term. The GPI data used to prepare this solution are drawn from the Global Peace Index web site.

Policy Implications of IEI Results: An Illustration

Among many foreseeable uses and theoretical implications too numerous to be delved into here, the IEI has applications for policy analysis and social planning on a macro scale. One such example is sustainability analysis followed by policy formulation as illustrated below. The purpose of this particular application is to identify which fundamental IEI factors should be the focus of national policy action in order to increase the rapidity of socioeconomic improvement within the country.

1) Comparing a nation's IEI ranking score with their <GDP-grpc ranking score is an indication of sustainability. For instance, the fact that a region such as the United Kingdom displays an IEI ranking score of 23 in contrast to a much higher <GDP-grpc ranking score of 4 suggests that the rapidity of <GDP is not being supported by current intellectual energy inputs and is therefore unsustainable over time. Conversely, a country such as Albania shows a high IEI ranking score of 6 and a middling <GDP score of 27, indicating that the country is able to sustain a faster rate of <GDP over time. Meanwhile, some nations such

as Finland score evenly (5,5) indicating that the <GDP there is stable and sustainable in the long run.

2) Now supposing policy makers in the UK were keen on becoming more sustainable by improving the IEI score. For this type of analysis we use a standardized multiple regression analysis. We see that the HDI variable exerts the largest influence with a coefficient of 1.30. However, the UK already scores high on the HDI (11) and bettering this score might prove difficult. The next strongest variable is the EPI (coefficient=-0.422), but here the UK scores even better (4). With Genetic Diversity (coefficient= -0.247) we reach a category in which the UK performs in the lowest quintile (44) and thus is illuminated one possible policy goal. Next comes Net Energy (coefficient= -0.235) and the UK performs in the fourth quintile here (37), indicating another possible policy target. GPI exerts the next strongest influence with a coefficient of 0.191, but again, the UK is among this sample's leaders (7). With Soil Sufficiency (coefficient= 0.102) the UK scores again in the lowest quintile (44). Finally, the GINI score (coefficient=.053) is moderately good at 14, leaving little room for improvement. Thus, based on this simulation using our limited group of nations and <GDP impact we would support the position that policies affecting Globality, Food Security, and Energy Security are most

needed to keep the UK a salubrious place to live far into the future.

INTELLECTUAL ENERGY INDEX (IEI)

Innocentive Challenge ID: 9932801

Supplementary Materials

Data

Indicators Used in External Indices Referred to in This Study

Formulas Used to Create Certain IEI Variables

IEI Raw Data, Scores, and Rankings

Other Raw Data, Scores, and Rankings

Data Used in Creating IEI Variables

Data Used in Creating GDP-grpc Variable

Multiple Regressions

IEI as 7 Independent Variables and GDP-grpc as Dependent Variable

IEI as 6 Independent Variables and GDP-grpc as Dependent Variable

Human Development Index Variables (Independent) and GDP-grpc as Dependent

Index Economic Freedom Variables (Independent) and GDP-grpc as Dependent

Democracy Index Variables (Independent) and GDP-grpc as Dependent Variable

IEI as 6 Independent Variables and HDI as Dependent Variable

Assumption Testing of IEI Variables

Normality

Outliers

Linearity

Multicollinearity

Theoretical Soundness

Heteroskedasticity

Indicators Used in External Indices Referred to in This Study

Human Development Index

1. School Life Expectancy
2. Mean School Years
3. Gross National Income per capita
4. Life Expectancy

Environmental Performance Index

1. Environmental Burden of Disease
2. Adequate Sanitation
3. Drinking Water
4. Indoor Air Pollution
5. Urban Particulates
6. Local Ozone
7. Regional Ozone
8. Sulfur Dioxide Emissions

9. Water Quality Index
10. Water Stress
11. Conservation Risk Index
12. Effective Conservation
13. Critical Habitat Protection
14. Marine Protected Areas
15. Growing Stock
16. Marine Trophic Index
17. Trawling Intensity
18. Irrigation Stress
19. Agricultural Subsidies
20. Intensive Cropland
21. Burnt Land Area
22. Pesticide Regulation
23. Emissions per capita
24. Emissions per electricity generated
25. Industrial carbon intensity

Global Peace Index

1. Number of external and internal wars fought
2. Estimated deaths due to external wars
3. Estimated deaths due to internal wars
4. Level of organized internal conflict
5. Relations with neighboring countries
6. Level of distrust in other citizens
7. Number of displaced persons as percentage of population
8. Political instability
9. Level of respect for human rights (political terror scale)
10. Potential for terrorist acts
11. Number of homicides
12. Level of violent crime
13. Likelihood of violent demonstration
14. Number of jailed persons

15. Number of police and security forces
16. Military expenditures as a percentage of GDP
17. Number of armed services personnel
18. Imports of major conventional weapons
19. Exports of major conventional weapons
20. United Nations deployments
21. Number of heavy weapons
22. Ease of access to small arms and light weapons
23. Military capability or sophistication

Democracy Index

1. Electoral process and pluralism
2. Functioning of government
3. Political participation
4. Political culture
5. Civil liberties

Index of Economic Freedom

1. Business Freedom
2. Trade Freedom
3. Fiscal Freedom
4. Gov't Spending
5. Monetary Freedom
6. Investment Freedom
7. Financial Freedom
8. Property Rights
9. Freedom From Corruption
10. Labor Freedom

Formulas Used to Create Certain IEI Variables

Soil Sufficiency Net Energy

SS=ln((T+A)/(1+(G+M)) NE=(P-C)/(1+(G+M))

Where,

SS is fertile soil statistic NE is net energy statistic
ln is log natural P is total energy production
T is forest land per person C is total energy consumption

A is arable land per person P is total population
G is population growth rate
M is net migration rate

Genetic Diversity

GD=(S1+S2)/2

or

GD=S1 NB: Second formula used pending completion of S2 data acquisition

Where,

GD is genetic diversity
S1 is the Shannon diversity statistic for Y-DNA haplogroups in population
S2 is the Shannon diversity statistic for mtDNA haplogroups in population

The Shannon diversity statistic is calculated as follows:

$$S = -\sum_{i=1}^{n} (p_i \ln p_i)$$

Where,

S is the Shannon diversity statistic
n is the total number of haplogroups
pi is the frequency of the *i*-th haplogroup
ln is log natural

[*This Space Intentionally Blank*]

IEI Raw Data, Scores, and Rankings

	HDI	Rnk	EPI	Rnk	NE	Rnk	GINI	Rnk	GD	Rnk	GPI	Rnk	SS	Rnk	IEI Score	IEI Rank
Afghanistan	0.3	47	32	50	-0.0003	14	60	47	0.7268	3	3.2	49	-1.2646	34	197	43
Albania	0.7	17	71	8	-0.0196	33	26.7	2	0.7003	7	1.9	17	-0.7979	26	108	6
Algeria	0.7	26	67	13	0.1726	1	35.3	17	0.5756	17	2.4	41	-1.2492	33	131	17
Argentina	0.8	14	61	25	0.0069	13	41.4	28	0.5688	19	1.9	15	0.3614	12	98	4
Armenia	0.7	23	60	27	-0.0577	39	37	19	0.686	8	2.3	32	-1.3439	37	166	30
Bangladesh	0.5	41	44	43	-0.0012	18	33.2	13	0.5748	18	2.1	25	-2.8274	49	194	42
Botswana	0.6	31	41	46	-0.0189	32	63	49	0.4428	34	1.7	10	1.7936	3	156	26
Brazil	0.7	21	63	19	-0.0101	30	56.7	44	0.5546	22	2	22	0.9596	7	121	11
Cambodia	0.5	38	42	45	-0.0044	25	43	32	0.5969	12	2.3	35	-0.0573	17	172	34
Canada	0.9	2	66	15	0.1474	4	32.1	10	0.4498	32	1.4	3	2.3216	1	57	1
Central African	0.3	48	33	49	-0.0009	17	61.3	48	0.5812	15	2.9	46	1.5842	4	179	38
China	0.7	27	49	36	-0.0044	26	41.5	29	0.3879	39	2.1	23	-1.3909	38	189	40
Colombia	0.7	24	77	2	0.0585	6	58.5	45	0.538	25	2.7	45	0.2668	13	115	8
Dominican Rep	0.7	27	68	12	-0.0278	34	49.9	40	0.5381	24	2.1	27	-1.3975	39	163	28
Egypt	0.6	32	62	23	0.0081	12	34.4	15	0.6392	10	2	21	-3.2381	50	148	25
Finland	0.9	7	75	3	-0.1516	49	26.8	3	0.4132	38	1.4	2	1.5376	5	104	5
France	0.9	6	78	1	-0.0937	43	32.7	11	0.4353	36	1.7	11	-1.2794	36	133	20
Germany	0.9	3	73	5	-0.1151	47	27	4	0.4822	30	1.4	4	-1.2714	35	124	15
Greece	0.9	9	61	26	-0.1004	44	33	12	0.6164	11	1.9	18	-0.5139	23	131	17
Haiti	0.4	44	39	47	-0.0029	22	59.2	46	0.2707	47	2.3	34	-2.4075	47	241	50
Hungary	0.8	12	69	11	-0.0720	40	24.7	1	0.4487	33	1.5	5	-0.4152	21	122	12
India	0.5	37	48	37	-0.0052	28	36.8	18	0.5305	26	2.6	42	-1.7281	43	213	47
Indonesia	0.6	33	45	42	0.0249	7	37	19	0.3868	40	2	19	-0.8305	27	168	31
Iran	0.7	20	60	29	0.0664	5	44.5	34	0.746	1	2.4	37	-1.0621	31	123	13
Italy	0.9	10	73	6	-0.1087	45	32	8	0.53	27	1.8	12	-1.2469	32	132	19
Japan	0.9	4	73	7	-0.1436	48	37.6	22	0.7068	6	1.3	1	0.0798	15	81	2
Kenya	0.5	40	51	33	-0.0037	23	42.5	31	0.287	46	2.3	33	-1.6337	42	217	49
South Korea	0.9	5	57	32	-0.1709	50	31.4	7	0.585	14	1.8	13	-0.9439	30	144	22
Liberia	0.3	50	43	44	-0.0025	21	52.6	43	0.1357	50	2.2	28	-0.1096	18	211	46
Mali	0.3	49	39	48	-0.0007	15	40.1	24	0.1695	48	2.2	30	0.1700	14	204	44
Mexico	0.8	15	67	14	0.0164	8	48.2	38	0.5782	16	2.4	38	-0.2562	19	110	7
Morocco	0.6	36	66	17	-0.0169	31	40.9	25	0.34	42	1.9	16	-0.8985	29	171	33
Pakistan	0.5	39	48	39	-0.0043	24	30.6	5	0.5892	13	2.9	47	-2.2207	46	208	45
Peru	0.7	16	69	10	-0.0049	27	49.6	39	0.7113	4	2.1	26	0.9012	8	91	3
Philippines	0.6	30	66	16	-0.0073	29	45.8	37	0.7098	5	2.6	43	-2.0578	45	168	31
Poland	0.8	13	63	20	-0.0321	36	34.9	16	0.3096	43	1.5	6	-0.5787	24	142	21
Russia	0.7	17	61	24	0.1712	2	42.2	30	0.5446	23	3	48	1.9403	2	116	9
South Africa	0.6	34	51	34	0.0091	11	65	50	0.4341	37	2.4	36	-0.7033	25	177	37
Spain	0.9	8	71	9	-0.1088	46	32	8	0.4378	35	1.6	8	-0.4100	20	126	16
Sudan	0.4	46	47	40	0.0156	9	51	42	0.6509	9	3.2	50	0.5964	10	164	29
Thailand	0.7	29	62	22	-0.0293	35	43	32	0.2898	45	2.2	31	-0.4365	22	184	39
Turkey	0.7	25	60	28	-0.0388	38	41	26	0.7281	2	2.4	40	-0.8803	28	161	27
Uganda	0.4	43	50	35	-0.0008	16	45.7	36	0.512	28	2.2	28	-1.5048	40	190	41
Ukraine	0.7	19	58	31	-0.0722	41	31	6	0.5673	20	2	20	-0.0556	16	147	23
United Kingdon	0.8	11	74	4	-0.0368	37	34	14	0.3072	44	1.6	7	-1.9743	44	147	23
United States o	0.9	1	63	18	-0.0855	42	45	35	0.5005	29	2.1	24	0.7518	9	123	13
Venezuela	0.7	22	63	21	0.1602	3	41	26	0.5552	21	2.4	39	0.5840	11	117	10
Viet Nam	0.6	35	59	30	-0.0016	19	37	19	0.371	41	1.7	9	-1.5245	41	175	35
Yemen	0.4	42	48	38	0.0125	10	37.7	23	0.477	31	2.7	44	-2.5519	48	213	47
Zambia	0.4	45	47	41	-0.0022	20	50.8	41	0.142	49	1.8	14	1.2003	6	175	35

Other Raw Data, Scores, and Rankings

Gross Development Product Data **Other Indices Used**

used to validate IEI variables individually and as multivariate index

	GDP-prpc	Rnk	DI	Rnk	IEF	Rnk
Afghanistan	74.10478	46	3.02	45	NA	NA
Albania	462.0442	27	5.91	27	64	19
Algeria	258.1137	35	3.32	43	52.4	38
Argentina	881.0802	16	6.63	21	51.7	41
Armenia	270.4103	34	4.09	40	69.7	9
Bangladesh	133.897	39	5.52	30	53	37
Botswana	1065.446	12	7.47	14	68.8	10
Brazil	673.419	19	7.38	16	56.3	30
Cambodia	184.7465	37	4.87	35	57.9	28
Canada	1008.644	13	9.07	2	80.8	1
Central African	37.50018	49	1.86	50	49.3	44
China	1076.023	11	3.04	44	52	40
Colombia	528.1734	25	6.54	22	68	12
Dominican Rep	579.4943	23	6.2	25	60	24
Egypt	346.7926	31	3.89	41	59.1	27
Finland	1243.618	5	9.25	1	74	4
France	1135.995	9	8.07	9	64.6	16
Germany	1382.224	3	8.82	3	71.8	6
Greece	1080.842	10	8.13	8	60.3	22
Haiti	97.24265	44	4.19	39	52.1	39
Hungary	1007.414	14	7.44	15	66.6	14
India	355.8499	30	7.8	13	54.6	35
Indonesia	376.955	29	6.34	23	56	33
Iran	426.4088	28	2.83	47	42.1	47
Italy	790.4565	17	7.98	11	60.3	22
Japan	1221.817	6	8.25	5	72.8	5
Kenya	101.0501	43	4.79	36	57.4	29
South Korea	1860.497	1	8.01	10	69.8	8
Liberia	27.28508	50	5.25	32	46.5	45
Mali	48.29362	48	5.87	28	56.3	30
Mexico	636.129	20	6.78	20	67.8	13
Morocco	304.3616	32	3.88	42	59.6	26
Pakistan	163.5276	38	4.46	38	55.1	34
Peru	634.994	21	6.31	24	68.6	11
Philippines	191.0214	36	6.12	26	56.2	32
Poland	1170.535	7	7.3	17	64.1	18
Russia	1169.004	8	4.48	37	50.5	43
South Africa	546.815	24	7.91	12	62.7	20
Spain	994.4704	15	8.45	4	70.2	7
Sudan	131.6838	41	2.81	48	NA	ERR
Thailand	610.9263	22	6.81	19	64.7	15
Turkey	690.9196	18	5.69	29	64.2	17
Uganda	66.96031	47	5.03	34	61.7	21
Ukraine	518.6666	26	6.94	18	45.8	46
United Kingdon	1273.417	4	8.15	7	74.5	3
United States o	1716.704	2	8.22	6	77.8	2
Venezuela	132.6865	40	5.34	31	37.6	48
Viet Nam	293.2644	33	2.53	49	51.6	42

Other Raw Data, Scores, and Rankings

	GDP-grpc	Rnk	DI	Rnk	IEF	Rnk
Yemen	80.60967	45	2.95	46	54.2	36
Zambia	123.1111	42	5.25	32	59.7	25

GDP-grpc (2011): Gross Domestic Product per capita (ppp) growth projected to 2016 (slope of regression x R^2) http://www.imf.org/external/pubs/ft/weo/2011/01/weodata/index.aspx

DI (2010): Democracy Index; http://graphics.eiu.com/PDF/Democracy_Index_2010_web.pdf

IEF (2011): Index of Economic Freedom; http://www.heritage.org/index/

HDI (2010): Human Development Index; http://hdr.undp.org/en/statistics/hdi/

EPI (2010): Environmental Performance Index; http://epi.yale.edu/

NE (2008): Net Energy, statistical variable created by Solver; see Other Data Used

GINI (various years): Gini Index, Distribution of Family Income; https://www.cia.gov/library/publications/the-world-factbook

GD (various years): Genetic Diversity, statistical variable created by Solver

GPI (2011): Global Peace Index; http://www.economicsandpeace.org/WhatWeDo/GPI

SS (2005-2007): Soil Sufficiency, statistical variable created by Solver; see Other Data Used

[This Space Intentionally Blank]

Data Used in Creating IEI Variables

	PopGro	PopActual	NetMig	EnerProd	EnerCon	Forest%	Arable%
Afghanistan	2.38	29.84	3.31	0.00789	0.01778	0.03	0.26
Albania	0.27	2.99	-3.34	0.05283	0.11139	0.27	0.18
Algeria	1.17	34.99	-0.27	7.81901	1.70987	0.07	0.22
Argentina	1.02	41.77	0	3.58566	3.2942	0.79	0.66
Armenia	0.06	2.97	-3.76	0.04497	0.2158	0.1	0.16
Bangladesh	1.57	158.57	-1.57	0.68074	0.87345	0.01	0.05
Botswana	1.66	2.07	4.82	0.02198	0.06202	5.96	0.18
Brazil	1.13	203.43	-0.09	8.54679	10.6296	2.35	0.29
Cambodia	1.7	14.7	-0.34	0.00052	0.06603	0.71	0.25
Canada	0.79	34.03	5.65	19.11366	14.0292	9.11	1.22
Central African	2.15	4.95	0	0.00128	0.00602	4.6	0.38
China	0.49	1336.72	-0.33	79.10769	85.0597	0.15	0.1
Colombia	1.16	44.73	-0.67	4.01611	1.37243	1.27	0.05
Dominican Rep	1.33	9.96	-2.01	0.01713	0.29675	0.14	0.11
Egypt	1.96	82.08	-0.21	3.85057	3.16914	0	0.04
Finland	0.08	5.26	0.62	0.4931	1.29176	4.28	0.38
France	0.5	65.31	1.46	5.12899	11.2903	0.14	0.14
Germany	-0.21	81.47	0.54	4.9925	14.3569	0.14	0.14
Greece	0.08	10.76	2.32	0.38596	1.46983	0.35	0.25
Haiti	0.79	9.72	-8.32	0.00176	0.02957	0.01	0.08
Hungary	-0.17	9.98	1.39	0.38743	1.1062	0.2	0.46
India	1.34	1189.17	-0.05	13.66393	19.9542	0.06	0.12
Indonesia	1.07	245.61	-1.15	11.9924	5.82233	0.36	0.08
Iran	1.25	77.89	-0.13	13.35475	8.12059	0.14	0.21
Italy	0.42	61.02	4.86	1.2059	7.89699	0.16	0.13
Japan	-0.28	126.48	0	3.76138	21.8737	1.05	0.03
Kenya	2.46	41.07	0	0.05436	0.20818	0.09	0.11
South Korea	0.23	48.75	0	1.53486	9.88495	0.14	0.25
Liberia	2.66	3.79	0	0	0.00957	0.83	0.09
Mali	2.61	14.16	-5.23	0.00271	0.01234	0.89	0.32
Mexico	1.1	113.72	-3.24	9.18396	7.30898	0.57	0.21
Morocco	1.07	31.97	-3.77	0.01513	0.55902	0.14	0.27
Pakistan	1.57	187.34	-2.17	1.65698	2.48147	0.01	0.1
Peru	1.03	29.25	-3.2	0.56098	0.69404	2.35	0.13
Philippines	1.9	101.83	-1.29	0.53457	1.293	0.07	0.06
Poland	-0.06	38.44	-0.47	2.65501	3.88691	0.24	0.32
Russia	-0.47	138.74	0.29	54.07118	30.4259	6.05	0.88
South Africa	-0.38	49	-6.19	6.1575	5.71413	0.19	0.3
Spain	0.57	46.75	3.89	1.36768	6.50467	0.38	0.29
Sudan	2.48	45.05	-0.29	0.90333	0.18862	1.5	0.36
Thailand	0.57	66.72	0	1.99275	3.95827	0.33	0.32
Turkey	1.24	78.79	0.51	1.20831	4.30511	0.13	0.29
Uganda	3.58	34.61	-0.02	0.01607	0.04367	0.11	0.12
Ukraine	-0.62	45.13	-0.09	3.06588	6.30195	0.22	0.72
United Kingdon	0.56	62.7	2.6	7.02189	9.34847	0.05	0.09
United States o	0.96	313.23	4.18	73.42271	100.578	0.97	1.18
Venezuela	1.49	27.64	0	7.68533	3.19277	1.73	0.09
Viet Nam	1.08	90.55	-0.35	1.4568	1.60524	0.15	0.07
Yemen	2.65	24.13	0	0.62513	0.31453	0.02	0.06
Zambia	3.06	13.88	-0.84	0.09432	0.12636	3.05	0.37

Data Used in Creating IEI Variables

PopGro (2011): Population Growth Rate; https://www.cia.gov/library/publications/the-world-factbook/index.html

PopActual (2011): Actual Population; https://www.cia.gov/library/publications/the-world-factbook/index.html

NetMig (2011): Net Migration; https://www.cia.gov/library/publications/the-world-factbook/index.html

EnerProd (2008): Energy Production; http://www.eia.doe.gov/cfapps/ipdbproject/IEDIndex3.cfm?tid=44&pid=44&aid=2

EnerCon (2008): Energy Consumption; http://www.eia.doe.gov/cfapps/ipdbproject/IEDIndex3.cfm?tid=44&pid=44&aid=2

Forest% (2007): Forest Area % of Land Area; FAO reported 2008: http://www.nationmaster.com

Arable% (2005, mostly): Arable % of Land Area; World Development Indicators reported 2008: http://www.nationmaster.com

Data Used in Creating GDP-grpc Variable

	IMF PROJECTED GDP per capita (ppp)								GDP-grpc
	2011	2012	2013	2014	2015	2016	Slope	RSquared	Slop X RSq
Afghanista	960.774	1016.3	1078.27	1149.34	1237.02	1340.29	75.166	0.98588162	74.10478
Albania	7752.53	8101.74	8507.84	8904.23	9510.29	10066.93	465.258286	0.99309177	462.0442
Algeria	7179.66	7404.79	7635.8	7890.8	8169.49	8484.31	259.21	0.99577061	258.1137
Argentina	16831.53	17682.47	18491.69	19341.43	20277.53	21282.24	882.527714	0.99835978	881.0802
Armenia	5349.92	5600.81	5862.43	6115.22	6403.3	6712.26	270.913143	0.99814372	270.4103
Bangladesh	1666.62	1775.67	1895.44	2029.88	2178.44	2340.43	134.622857	0.99460792	133.897
Botswana	16374.56	17467.53	18721.61	19716.95	20838.08	21636.43	1069.03829	0.99664006	1065.446
Brazil	11767.16	12320.79	12892.23	13527.7	14328.54	15193.35	679.704857	0.9907521	673.419
Cambodia	2251.14	2405.66	2568.95	2752.1	2958.41	3183.12	185.751429	0.99459005	184.7465
Canada	39981.63	40978.46	41913.55	42837.55	43919.85	45108.04	1010.86343	0.99780433	1008.644
Central Africa	764.574	794.01	827.739	867.82	907.457	952.304	37.6877714	0.99502261	37.50018
China	8288.82	9157.41	10103.25	11172.77	12374.79	13729.03	1083.506	0.99309393	1076.023
Colombia	9997.6	10467.99	10944.92	11467.75	12040.94	12657.9	529.805143	0.99692003	528.1734
Dominican Re	9257.43	9726.27	10257.78	10838.9	11477.12	12166.17	582.210571	0.99533457	579.4943
Egypt	6361.05	6575.1	6855.37	7229.41	7639.93	8120.66	353.330857	0.98149526	346.7926
Finland	35885.07	37100.47	38219.21	39447.92	40771.3	42154.32	1245.35571	0.99860454	1243.618
France	34858.09	35804.82	36821.07	37962.81	39222.56	40567.71	1141.23029	0.99541257	1135.995
Germany	37429.52	38815.32	40133.75	41530.74	42917.77	44364.83	1382.454	0.99983378	1382.224
Greece	27843.94	28503.47	29449.77	30490.58	31810.54	33370.7	1102.73771	0.98014434	1080.842
Haiti	1258.58	1366.39	1460.52	1556.37	1651.39	1749.37	97.28	0.99961606	97.24265
Hungary	19501.34	20353.62	21224.39	22224.35	23362.23	24589.19	1013.28686	0.99420434	1007.414
India	3608.2	3892.75	4213.95	4571.11	4965.31	5398.34	357.872571	0.9943482	355.8499
Indonesia	4657.13	4963.63	5295.34	5675.86	6096.57	6555.61	379.192571	0.99409901	376.955
Iran	10797.94	11086.84	11433.3	11890.36	12399.43	12945.13	432.308	0.98635408	426.4088
Italy	29888.87	30563.78	31253	32032.74	32917.74	33884.25	794.814857	0.99451657	790.4565
Japan	34645.99	35907.13	37054.95	38254.61	39499.75	40806.32	1222.262	0.99963576	1221.817
Kenya	1725.09	1810.26	1903.29	2005.42	2115.1	2231.43	101.381429	0.99673233	101.0501
South Korea	31410.47	33072.46	34784.89	36612.5	38616	40777.07	1865.46371	0.99733754	1860.497
Liberia	405.059	436.689	463.976	483.788	522.425	541.831	27.4537143	0.9938576	27.28508
Mali	1302.58	1350.67	1392.52	1439.16	1491.29	1547.8	48.4171429	0.99744882	48.29362
Mexico	15113.93	15782.9	16357.4	16965.76	17634.43	18338.93	636.798571	0.99894849	636.129
Morocco	4939.69	5183.3	5453.74	5751.1	6110.01	6468.28	306.298286	0.99367701	304.3616
Pakistan	2851.06	2957.08	3094.59	3261.07	3461.09	3678.48	166.160286	0.98415579	163.5276
Peru	9965.14	10548.52	11122.59	11750.45	12439.67	13183.99	637.016	0.99682581	634.994
Philippines	3890.19	4060.99	4234.09	4422.96	4630.01	4852.04	191.576571	0.99710217	191.0214
Poland	19887.28	20889.24	21949.79	23089.41	24390.3	25787.81	1175.58429	0.99570474	1170.535
Russia	16840.8	17904.35	18986.14	20152.22	21385.71	22717.46	1171.24171	0.99808934	1169.004
South Africa	10855.77	11292.95	11773.47	12326.62	12943.72	13606.56	550.268857	0.99372327	546.815
Spain	30233.77	31067.86	31954.52	32978.99	34073.36	35213.74	998.309143	0.99615472	994.4704
Sudan	2570.87	2681.95	2802.92	2928.74	3077.8	3234.18	132.283429	0.99546726	131.6838
Thailand	9598.01	10110	10657.1	11260.53	11934.63	12681	614.064857	0.99488886	610.9263
Turkey	14076.93	14742.27	15370.16	16046	16778.85	17564.31	692.070857	0.99833647	690.9196
Uganda	1263.28	1337.37	1398.99	1466.23	1539.95	1619.14	67.2651429	0.99546825	66.96031
Ukraine	7126.07	7616.29	8101.7	8609.63	9151.19	9739.24	519.385143	0.99861652	518.6660
United Kingdo	35645.8	36731.81	37879.13	39134.92	40545.95	42058.02	1278.83743	0.99576156	1273.417
United States -	48665.81	50273.2	51810.46	53499.31	55361.15	57319.74	1720.63657	0.99771311	1716.704
Venezuela	11930.86	12045.78	12119.76	12248.31	12430.69	12631.26	136.721714	0.9704859	132.6865
Viet Nam	3326.31	3557.11	3817.27	4112.26	4441.88	4803.17	295.245714	0.99328935	293.2644
Yemen	2635.92	2699.16	2769.61	2849.83	2940.98	3043.62	81.2622857	0.99196908	80.60967
Zambia	1592.82	1692.2	1803.31	1928.65	2069.79	2206.78	123.654571	0.99560486	123.1111

Multiple Regression Showing IEI as 7 Independent Variables and GDP-grpc as Dependent Variable
unstandardized and standardized

Regression Statistics	
Multiple R	0.934372
R Square	0.873051
Adjusted R Square	0.851892
Standard Error (Unstand)	184.5735
Observations	50

ANOVA (Unstand)

	df	*SS*	*MS*	*F*	*Significance F*
Regression	7	9840027	1405718	41.26289	8.06E-017
Residual	42	1430830	34067.37		
Total	49	11270856			

Unstandard	*Coefficients*	*Standard Error*	*t Stat*	*P-value*	*Lower 99.0%*	*Upper 99.0%*
Intercept	-840.273	322.0974	-2.60876	0.012534	-1709.31	28.76815
HDI	3529.754	345.8932	10.20475	6.1E-013	2596.509	4462.998
EPI	-16.8001	4.068153	-4.12966	0.000169	-27.7763	-5.82392
Net Energy	-1543.94	434.502	-3.55336	0.000956	-2716.26	-371.626
GINI	2.506117	3.422258	0.732299	0.468053	-6.72738	11.73961
Genetic Diversity	-768.616	223.7858	-3.4346	0.001348	-1372.41	-164.826
GPI	197.3895	100.4679	1.964701	0.056087	-73.6801	468.4591
Soil Sufficiency	38.14948	24.13481	1.580683	0.121453	-26.9679	103.2669

Standardized	*Coefficients*	*Standard Error*	*t Stat*	*P-value*	*Lower 99.0%*	*Upper 99.0%*
Intercept	-5.4E-016	0.054426	-1.00E-014	1	-0.14684	0.146844
HDI	1.304303	0.127813	10.20475	6.1E-013	0.959454	1.649153
EPI	-0.42254	0.102318	-4.12966	0.000169	-0.6986	-0.14648
Net Energy	-0.23576	0.066347	-3.55336	0.000956	-0.41477	-0.05675
GINI	0.053708	0.073341	0.732299	0.468053	-0.14417	0.251587
Genetic Diversity	-0.24723	0.071982	-3.4346	0.001348	-0.44144	-0.05302
GPI	0.191137	0.097286	1.964701	0.056087	-0.07135	0.453621
Soil Sufficiency	0.102028	0.064547	1.580683	0.121453	-0.07212	0.276181

Some might argue that the Soil Sufficiency and especially the GINI variables are not significant enough to be included in this index. However, the dependent variable here, GDP growth, is not the same socioeconomic quality as intellectual energy and therefore I posit, subject to further validation, that these variables are significant for purposes of measuring intellectual energy. Nevertheless, I also include the possibility of omitting the GINI from the regression, as shown below. In the six variable index all variables are significant when regressed against GDP growth. Either the seven or six variable IEI may be used to measure intellectual energy potential with similar results.

[This Space Intentionally Blank]

Multiple Regression Showing IEI as 6 Independent Variables and GDP-grpc as Dependent Variable

unstandardized and standardized

Regression Statistics	
Multiple R	0.933504
R Square	0.87143
Adjusted R Square	0.85349
Standard Error (Unstand)	183.5755
Observations	50

ANOVA (Unstand)

	df	*SS*	*MS*	*F*	*Significance F*
Regression	6	9821758	1636960	48.57452	1.43E-017
Residual	43	1449099	33699.97		
Total	49	11270856			

Unstandard	*Coefficients*	*Standard Error*	*t Stat*	*P-value*	*Lower 99.0%*	*Upper 99.0%*
Intercept	-731.848	284.5034	-2.57237	0.013637	-1498.61	34.91848
HDI	3486.445	338.957	10.2858	3.64E-013	2572.92	4399.97
EPI	-16.9518	4.040905	-4.19506	0.000134	-27.8425	-6.06117
Net Energy	-1558.14	431.7225	-3.60912	0.000796	-2721.68	-394.599
GPI	216.661	96.43583	2.246685	0.029848	-43.2438	476.5657
Genetic Diversity	-777.537	222.2457	-3.49855	0.001101	-1376.51	-178.562
Soil Sufficiency	45.22434	21.99718	2.055916	0.045894	-14.0604	104.5091

Standardized	*Coefficients*	*Standard Error*	*t Stat*	*P-value*	*Lower 99.0%*	*Upper 99.0%*
Intercept	-5.5E-016	0.054131	-1.00E-014	1	-0.14589	0.14589
HDI	1.2883	0.12525	10.2858	3.64E-013	0.950737	1.625863
EPI	-0.42636	0.101633	-4.19506	0.000134	-0.70027	-0.15244
Net Energy	-0.23792	0.065923	-3.60912	0.000796	-0.41559	-0.06025
GPI	0.209798	0.093381	2.246685	0.029848	-0.04187	0.461471
Genetic Diversity	-0.2501	0.071486	-3.49855	0.001101	-0.44276	-0.05744
Soil Sufficiency	0.12095	0.05883	2.055916	0.045894	-0.0376	0.279503

Multiple Regression Showing Human Development Index Variables (Independent) and GDP-grpc as Dependent

unstandarized only

Regression Statistics	
Multiple R	0.8971324
R Square	0.8048465
Adjusted R Square	0.7874995
Standard Error	221.08558
Observations	50

ANOVA

	df	*SS*	*MS*	*F*	*Significance F*
Regression	4	9071308.76957	2267827.19	46.396919	2.063994E-015
Residual	45	2199547.42139	48878.8316		
Total	49	11270856.191			

	Coefficients	*Standard Error*	*t Stat*	*P-value*	*Lower 99.0%*	*Upper 99.0%*
Intercept	-110.4363	275.743634883	-0.4005035	0.6906808	-852.07475995	631.2021536
SchoolExpec	23.146501	20.8554951887	1.10985141	0.2729588	-32.946316406	79.23931771
GNIpc	0.0226397	0.00448098482	5.05238809	0.0000077	0.01058764395	0.034691705
LifeExpec	-2.599076	4.91030645995	-0.5293104	0.5991917	-15.805807775	10.60765491
MeanYrSchool	41.97109	21.0537067111	1.99352498	0.0522868	-14.654835369	98.59701584

Multiple Regression Showing Index Economic Freedom Variables (Independent) and GDP-grpc as Dependent
unstandarized only

Regression Statistics	
Multiple R	0.7999585
R Square	0.6399336
Adjusted R Square	0.5426184
Standard Error	323.39042
Observations	48

No data available for Afghanistan and Sudan

ANOVA

	df	*SS*	*MS*	*F*	*Significance F*
Regression	10	6877147.84928	687714.785	6.5758827	0.0000944354
Residual	37	3869510.49923	104581.365		
Total	47	10746658.3485			

	Coefficients	*Standard Error*	*t Stat*	*P-value*	*Lower 99.0%*	*Upper 99.0%*
Intercept	-163.9279	860.647572769	-0.1904704	0.8499818	-2500.9350728	2173.079356
Business Freedom	1.3108232	5.01067372011	0.26160618	0.7950759	-12.295188131	14.91683454
Trade Freedom	4.0032194	9.16956845037	0.43657664	0.6649556	-20.895877873	28.90231664
Fiscal Freedom	1.844399	7.49167703556	0.24619307	0.8068935	-18.498542588	22.18734054
Gov't Spending	-1.542081	3.80280538327	-0.4055113	0.6874371	-11.868239449	8.784078401
Monetary Freedom	-2.332529	10.0583991726	-0.2318986	0.8178946	-29.645162238	24.98010407
Investment Freedom	-2.565652	4.98370911248	-0.5148076	0.6097493	-16.098443014	10.96713997
Financial Freedom	-1.071818	5.66651243929	-0.1891494	0.8510095	-16.458697011	14.31506189
Property Rights	6.4434396	8.5388005275	0.75460711	0.4552612	-16.74266695	29.6297461
Freedom from Corruption	12.431986	9.11100808296	1.36450168	0.1806517	-12.308096237	37.17206798
Labor Freedom	-0.893089	3.78459350255	-0.2359802	0.8147494	-11.169795524	9.383617041

Multiple Regression Showing Democracy Index Variables (Independent) and GDP-grpc as Dependent Variable
unstandarized only

Regression Statistics	
Multiple R	0.7565293
R Square	0.5723365
Adjusted R Square	0.5237384
Standard Error	330.9811
Observations	50

ANOVA

	df	*SS*	*MS*	*F*	*Significance F*
Regression	5	6450722.61714	1290144.52	11.776927	0.0000029352
Residual	44	4820133.57382	109548.49		
Total	49	11270856.191			

	Coefficients	*Standard Error*	*t Stat*	*P-value*	*Lower 99.0%*	*Upper 99.0%*
Intercept	-583.1247	181.485294862	-3.2130687	0.0024587	-1071.7350758	-94.5143602
I Electoral process and pluralism	-29.60515	46.2394752376	-0.6402571	0.5253258	-154.0950628	94.88475085
II Functioning of government	63.379854	35.320912699	1.79440022	0.0796217	-31.714152711	158.4738601
III Political participation	119.63784	51.2065714121	2.3363767	0.0240903	-18.224906051	257.5005867
IV Political culture	62.998594	43.1227976883	1.46091157	0.1511445	-53.100319622	179.097508
V Civil liberties	18.167048	57.212056964	0.31753881	0.7523368	-135.86418389	172.1982808

Multiple Regression Showing IEI as 6 Independent Variables and HDI as Dependent Variable
unstandarized only
HDI omitted as Independent Variable to avoid collinearity with HDI as Dependent Variable

Regression Statistics	
Multiple R	0.9039537
R Square	0.8171323
Adjusted R Square	0.7916158
Standard Error	0.0808997
Observations	50

ANOVA

	df	*SS*	*MS*	*F*	*Significance F*
Regression	6	1.25752839498	0.20958807	32.023774	2.462561E-014
Residual	43	0.28142488502	0.00654476		
Total	49	1.53895328			

	Coefficients	*Standard Error*	*t Stat*	*P-value*	*Lower 99.0%*	*Upper 99.0%*
Intercept	0.4273888	0.12857691343	3.32399369	0.0018206	0.08086048367	0.773917215
EPI	0.0074377	0.00139030533	5.3496748	0.0000032	0.00369066164	0.011184701
Net Energy	0.0000402	0.00002647477	1.51876515	0.1361407	-0.0000311433	0.000111561
GINI	-0.001823	0.00145935098	-1.2493502	0.2182951	-0.0057563456	0.002109865
Genetic Diversity	0.2663309	0.08437668994	3.15645111	0.002916	0.03892680287	0.49373499
GPI	-0.118978	0.03345236693	-3.5566438	0.0009293	-0.2091358163	-0.02882049
Soil Sufficiency	0.0208998	0.00972242389	2.14965391	0.0372515	-0.005303113	0.047102806

[*This Space Intentionally Blank*]

Assumption Testing of IEI Variables

Normality

calculated on Wessa.net

Variable	Kurtosis	SE	Ratio
HDI	-0.864911	0.661908	1.306693679
EPI	-0.795093	0.661908	1.201213764
NE	1.390603	0.661908	**2.100900729**
GINI	-0.369685	0.661908	0.558514174
GD	-0.185041	0.661908	0.279556978
GPI	-0.034425	0.661908	0.052008738
SS	0.325462	0.661908	0.491702774

Variable	Skewness	SE	Ratio
HDI	-0.37651	0.336601	1.11856471
EPI	-0.393097	0.336601	1.167842639
NE	0.531762	0.336601	1.579799228
GINI	0.601789	0.336601	1.787840797
GD	-0.535299	0.336601	1.590307218
GPI	0.452436	0.336601	1.344131479
SS	0.276349	0.336601	0.820998749

Outliers

Means and standard deviations calculated for each variable
Outlier defined as greater than +/-3 SD from mean
No outliers detected

Linearity

Plots for all variables have been inspected for linearity and they appear linear.

Multicollinearity

Corrleation Table (R Squared) for all Independent Variables
BOLD–p < .05

	HDI	EPI	NE	GINI	GD	GPI	SS
HDI	1						
EPI	**0.690677423**	1					
NE	**-0.10954062**	-0.0407805	1				
GINI	**-0.25924142**	**-0.2246957**	**0.085497183**	1			
GD	0.054812725	0.03121373	0.000279849	-0.002594	1		
GPI	**-0.37078201**	**-0.2415528**	**0.224459885**	**0.2344256**	0.0718543	1	
SS	0.028626077	0.00275727	0.023921474	0.0667991	0.0046883	0.00626662	1

Assumption Testing of IEI Variables

<u>Theoretical Soundness</u>

Theoretical Impact of Variables on IEI

Variable	*Scale Direction*	*Interpretation*
HDI	Higher is better	More human developlent means more intellectual energy
EPI	Higher is better	Better environmental performance means more intellectual energy
Net Energy	Higher is better	More energy security means more intellectual energy
GINI	Lower is better	More equal income distribution means more intellectual energy
Genetic Diversi	Higher is better	More genetic variability means more intellectual energy
GPI	Lower is better	More peace and democracy means more intellectual energy
Soil Sufficiency	Higher is better	More food security means more intellectual energy

Correlation of Individual Variables with GDP-grpc to 2016 (not as multivariate model)

IEI Variable	*R-Squared*	*Significance*
HDI	0.7161647	1.00E-014
EPI	0.3028822	3.46E-005
Net Energy	0.214685	0.000703
GINI	0.1198346	0.013795
Genetic Diversi	0.000907	0.835527
GPI	0.327552	1.41E-005
Soil Sufficiency	0.051772	0.112028

Non-IEI Variabl	*R-Squared*	*Significance*
GNIpc (ppp)	0.659608	8.18E-013

Theoretical Impact of IEI Variables on GDP-prc to 2016

Multiple Regression Equation (Unstandardized)

$$GDP\text{-}prc = -840.273 + HDI*3529.75 + EPI*-16.8 + NE*-1543 + GINI*2.50 + GD*-768.61 + GPI*197.38 + SS*38.14$$

Multiple Regression Equation (Standardized)

$$GDP\text{-}prc = -5.4E\text{-}16 + HDI*1.3 + EPI*-0.42 + NE*-0.23 + GINI*0.05 + GD*-0.24 + GPI*0.19 + SS*0.1$$

Variable	*Scale Direction*	*% Impact on GDI-prc to 2016*
HDI	Higher is better	51.38%
EPI	Higher is better	-16.60%
Net Energy	Higher is better	-9.09%
GINI	Lower is better	-1.98%
Genetic Diversi	Higher is better	-9.49%
GPI	Lower is better	-7.51%
Soil Sufficiency	Higher is better	3.95%

Variable	*Interpretation for GDP-prc to 2016 regression*
HDI	Current state of human development has strongest impact on GDP growth in short term
EPI	Better environmental performance lowers GDP growth in short term
Net Energy	Greater energy security lowers GDP growth in short term
GINI	More equal income distribution lowers GDP growth in short term
Genetic Diversi	More genetic variability lowers GDP growth in short term
GPI	More peace and democracy lowers GDP growth in short term
Soil Sufficiency	More food security increases GDP growth in short term

Assumption Testing of IEI Variables

Theoretical Soundness, cont

Discussion

The GDP-prc to 2016 interpretations may suggest to some that only HDI (education, health, income) and Soil Sufficiency are policies worth pursuing. All the other factors seem to have a negative impact on GDP growth. This may seem counter-intuitive but is explained by three important considerations:

a) the five year study period is not long enough for most of the factors to cause their effect,

b) GDP growth is not the only desired effect of intellectual energy, and

c) these braking forces, by slowing GDP growth to sustainable levels, prevent socioeconomic collapse

The IEI is a measure of the group's potential to sustain or improve upon current socioeconomic performance in the short, medium, and long terms. Five year GDP growth is only one aspect of overall performance. These results help explain why issues like the environment, energy, income, diversity, democracy, and peace are so often given a lower priority in national and international policy making when short-term GDP statistics are viewed as the main weather vane of success. Policy-makers should understand that medium to long term GDP success may require some near-term GDP sacrifices and that uncontrolled growth can be harmful.

Heteroskedasticity

Goldfeld-Quandt test for Heteroskedasticity

calculated on Wessa.net

p-values	Alternative Hypothesis		
breakpoint index	greater	2-sided	less
11	0.3925475	0.785095	0.6074525
12	0.5267436	0.946513	0.4732564
13	0.3753577	0.750715	0.6246423
14	0.2528964	0.505793	0.7471036
15	0.1878675	0.375735	0.8121325
16	0.157411	0.314822	0.842589
17	0.0952874	0.190575	0.9047126
18	0.1322959	0.264592	0.8677041
19	0.0945228	0.189046	0.9054772
20	0.3629498	0.7259	0.6370502
21	0.2819444	0.563889	0.7180556
22	0.2148092	0.429618	0.7851908
23	0.2833765	0.566753	0.7166235
24	0.2074115	0.414823	0.7925885
25	0.3165423	0.633085	0.6834577
26	0.2444339	0.488868	0.7555661
27	0.201476	0.402952	0.798524
28	0.435271	0.870542	0.564729
29	0.3633725	0.726745	0.6366275
30	0.2921121	0.584224	0.7078879
31	0.2199848	0.43997	0.7800152
32	0.1538408	0.307682	0.8461592
33	0.1011477	0.202295	0.8988523
34	0.0616699	0.12334	0.9383301
35	0.0537658	0.107532	0.9462342
36	0.0664046	0.132809	0.9335954
37	0.1523308	0.304662	0.8476692
38	0.2749549	0.54991	0.7250451
39	0.2403857	0.480771	0.7596143

Assumption Testing of IEI Variables

<u>Heteroskedasticity, cont.</u>

Meta Analysis of Goldfeld-Quandt test for Heteroskedasticity

Description	# significant tests	% significant tests	OK/NOK
1% type I error level	0	0	OK
5% type I error level	0	0	OK
10% type I error level	0	0	OK

[*This Space Intentionally Blank*]

REMATERIALIZING EVERYDAY LIFE

Projects: 1) Glycerine Soap Recycler; 2) From Tree Books to E-AudioBooks

Entrepreneurial Platform(s): Internet Website Commerce; Quirky.com; Huddle

Submitted: 9/13/2010 and 5/22/2011

Background and Description

Much of my ideation during the designing year involved looking around the house and asking myself how I could make everyday objects and supplies more environmentally sustainable. This usually involves thinking about how I to substitute new materials and technologies for these objects. The soap recycler idea originated from several sources. For many years I had been wondering how I might use those tiny end slivers of soap that are too small to manage comfortably and for many years I filed this thought away for later use. Meanwhile I had been reading about proposed uses for the large amounts of glycerine produced as waste during the biodiesel production process. Then last year, I came across some research establishing that certain compounds found in broccoli had strong anti-skin cancer properties. I also learned that the lymphatic circulatory system lacks a pump and so the distribution around the body of this immunity requires physical activity or massage. Around that time I had also tried a soap cake embedded with fleck of kelp that I found to provide ideal scrubbing massage action for the lymphatic system. I searched around for a soap combining these elements and was unable to find one. So putting all of this together, I invented a device that would allow the user to mix some waste glycerine and beeswax, along with unusable soap chips and slivers, if desired, add any other compounds (such as broccoli powder, kelp, tea-tree oil, fragrances, and colors), cook the mixture in a microwave for a few minutes and then pour into a mold for a quick solidification in the freezer. The product consists of the cooker/mold system, the glycerine, the beeswax, and instruction on how to add other ingredients. Additional supplies of glycerine and beeswax would be made available. I have made numerous bars of my own anti-cancer soap, confident that I know exactly what ingredients and chemicals are in this material that I apply to my skin everyday and making use of a biodiesel by-product that might otherwise become waste. The product was proposed on Quirky.com, an invention development community, but lost out to a combination stool/beer cooler concept.

Along a similar line of thought, for many years I had been looking around my apartment to notice that my bookshelves were becoming more and more crowded. A few years ago I began scanning books into digital form in order to make more space. Then one day my collaborator, the engineer Ryuhei Ishikawa, said he had seen a company in Japan that was offering to scan books into digital files and that it had caught on well. He wanted to create such an internet book-scanning company here. After some skepticism that anyone really reads anymore, I agreed to help. I provided legal and editorial support for the company's web site and also contributed the audio conversion capabilities for the service. Using an audio conversion system I had developed over the years for my own use (a tweaked-up version of a commercially available text-to-speech engine), the audio service allows customers to submit any text and receive an mp3 file of that text read by state-of-the-art speech readers. This is provided at a very reasonable price of $8.50 per 300 page book, Of course, customers may also choose to scan their old books for their e-readers as well. The commercial web site is located here: http://bookscan.us/service-detail.html (*scroll down to' mp3 Format' for audio services*).

Several other dematerialization concepts never got from the hopper to the drawing board last year and I mention them here for a rainy day: 1) Solar Tree/Gadget Battery Charger: the idea is to have a constant supply of solar charged batteries of all sizes for all those little gadgets. There is thin film PV technology that could allow the formation of leaves and stems and bark that is all PV surfaced so that the tree could actually be fairly small with lots of solar active area. The kit would include the tree, a battery charger, wiring to connect the tree to the charger inside the home, and tree planting instructions (the tree could also be 'planted' indoors in a sunny corner). A similar variation would be a weather vane that includes both PV and a small wind turbine that is also for charging gadget batteries; 2) Kitchen Scraps to Fuel System: this appliance takes in kitchen scraps and turns them into fuel pellets (using heat-assisted composting and a press) for a small portable biomass gasifying cookstove (for camping, car, emergency, etc) or in the alternative, the device is a bioreactor/microbial fuel cell where methanogenic microbes power a fuel cell connected to a gadget battery recharger; 3) Home CO_2 Capture to Fuel Reactor: this appliance captures atmospheric CO_2 using a technology invented by my collaborator, the engineer Ryuhei Ishikawa, and then uses either a catalytic conversion process (for instance: http://wp.me/p6rKuZ-13Q) or a microbial process where natural or engineered microbes or photosynthesizers feed on the CO_2 and produce bio-gas or bio-oil. For home use it seems that catalytic conversion is closer than microbes; 4) Home Aquatic Poly-Culture System: this appliance brings Polynesian pond poly-culture into a corner of the home. A small largely self-sustaining system could produce aquatic plants and algae, small fish and crustaceans, filter feeding bivalves, and bottom feeding mollusks. Each of these products could be harvested for food accenting or spicing.

GEO-ENGINEERING QUOTIDIAN GEOLOGICAL PROCESSES AND CYCLES

Projects: Soil Nitrate Capture System

Entrepreneurial Platform(s): Innocentive Challenge

Submitted: 5/26/2011

Background

I am a supporter of the application, acceleration, and/or stimulation of natural processes to solve environmental problems. This is a form of geo-engineering, yes, but not quite the same as, say, seeding the atmosphere with large quantities of sulphur dioxide to block the sun or diverting rivers to bring water to arid zones. Acceptable forms of geo-engineering involve the ramping up of naturally occurring, everyday processes so that they function at a higher rate. This is something like boosting the immune system of an organism so that it is better equipped to fight off disease (e.g., vitamin C, etc.). The earlier described Sustainable Global Change Infrastructure is an example of this: bicarbonate is a natural constituent of sea water, by adding more we are simply boosting the carbon mineralization that is taking place all the time.

This challenge sought concepts and designs that would enable growers to cost effectively capture nitrates from tile-drain effluent before being emitted to the environment. I had always been a supporter of the agricultural use of pyrogenic carbon (char) as a soil additive. Then I stumbled upon a research report stating that char also displays potent nitrate capturing properties. This appealed to me as the perfect solution to this challenge since the char could be created on-site from agricultural wastes, could be applied by the farmer using existing equipment, would not only capture nitrates but also enhance productivity, and would last a long time before requiring replenishment.

The Challenge

The Seeker wishes to receive concepts and designs that would enable growers to cost effectively capture nitrates from tile drain effluent before it is emitted to the environment. Such an "end of pipe" solution would supplement other best practices that are being deployed to reduce excess nitrogen use in agriculture and preventing it's efflux to neighboring environments. Potential solutions could include filtration technologies, tile drain management procedures, or other approaches.

Ease of use and robustness is extremely important in agricultural workflows and so any proposed method should require infrequent maintenance and be functional at a wide range of environmental temperatures.

The Seeker requests solutions that would be amenable to fulfilling the following Technical Requirements:

* Compatible with tile drain systems

* Efficient (>40%) capture of nitrates from tile drain effluents

* Cost less than establishing a wetland and/or reduce the amount of land removed from production to generate the same benefits.

* Be low maintenance & robust

* Remain viable during periods without fresh drainage water (dry weather)

* Captured nitrates are amenable to use by growers (application to farmland)

The Solution

PYROGENIC CARBON AMENDMENT

Innocentive Challenge ID: 9932805

Summary

This solution presents a nitrate capture system consisting of tile drain management by means of a pre-pipe soil amendment of pyrogenic carbon. The capture material is not only effective in trapping and holding nitrates but produces numerous ancillary benefits to create a low-cost, low-maintenance, and environmentally sustainable solution. The system may be implemented into new installations or retrofitted to existing tile drain systems.

Description

Pyrogenic carbon, sometimes referred to as biochar, is the product of the incomplete combustion of biomass. This material may be purchased on the open market, or may be produced locally from agricultural wastes[46] or other types of biomass. With the aid of a leased, mobile pyrolysis reactor,[47] individual farms could periodically produce, store, and incorporate char made from their own wastes and thus further enhance the cost-benefit equation in their favor. Numerous studies have shown that adding biochar to soil: 1) improves water retention, 2) reduces erosion, 3) decreases density, 4) retains heavy metals, 5) reduces salinity, and 6) increases healthy soil microbiota.[48] These benefits have been proven to increase agricultural production yields while lowering input costs.[49] However, the main property of biochar that is relevant to this solution is its ability to mitigate nitrate leaching from soil.[50] This property not only avoids run-off pollution into waterways, but by reducing the need for nitrogenous and other fertilizer inputs, reduces the energy, pollution, and economic costs associated with fertilizer production and application.[51]

Installation of pyrogenic carbon begins with the selection of the proper combustion protocol to create the most advantageous species of biochar. Studies have shown that slow pyrolysis is the most suitable method to produce a char for agricultural soil amendment.[52], [53] The char product is then ground to a coarse powder and may be applied to the soil in any of various ways, depending on the demands and options available in a given installation.[54] For new installations or drain improvement situations, the char may be incorporated as a structural layer just above the tile drain stratum. In fields where tile drains have already been installed, the char may be incorporated using any plowing method. It may be mixed with other soil amendments such as lime, manure, compost, biosolids, and so on, or it may be injected alone into trenches using equipment such as a subsurface banding machine. The ideal incorporation depth for the char is from just below the surface to 3 feet, which coordinates well with the placement of tile drains from 3 to 4.5 feet below the surface.

The application rate of the char will vary depending on environmental factors and must be determined on a case by case basis, requiring technical expertise and professional consultation. Factors such as the amount of nitrogenous fertilizer inputs, precipitation rates, crop type, and many others will affect the char's action. However, based on prior studies, the amount of char required is expected to be somewhere between 1 and 40 tons per acre. The char may be incorporated incrementally at any rate over any area. No foreseeable maintenance is required on the char portion of the system (tile drains will require the usual oversight). If done properly, that is, if the char is produced locally by slow pyrolysis from agricultural wastes using leased equipment and applied so as to reduce irrigation and fertilization costs and raise productivity, the net costs of implementation should be small or even negative. A simple water test at the tile drain outfalls will indicate when it is time to replenish the char. Since biochar has a half-life of over 1,000 years,[55] soil replenishment needs should be minimal after the initial incorporation, presuming that the initial environmental factors remain the same. Incremental replenishment may be performed by means of any incorporation method at any time.

Technical Requirement Compliance

Compatible with tile drain systems

Pyrogenic char incorporation is completely consistent with new or existing tile drain systems. The soil strata for char incorporation (0 to 3 feet) are above the typical depths of drain pipe installation (3 to 4.5 feet). The char action will reduce the hydrological load on to the drain system as well as prevent the leaching out of nitrates into the drain system.

Efficient (>40%) capture of nitrates from tile drain effluents

There is no doubt that biochar is capable of capturing close to 100% of excess nitrates produced by agricultural cultivation. A recent study tested this proposition and found that the char amendments to fields fertilized with biosolids produced the same amount of nitrate runoff, or even less, than the control fields where no nitrogen fertilizers were added.[56]

Cost less than establishing a wetland and/or reduce the amount of land removed from production to generate the same benefits

The cost of biochar soil amendment is a function of the amount of char needed, the source of the char, the input savings in areas such as irrigation and fertilizer caused by the char, the production improvements stimulated by the char, and the minimal costs of subsequent maintenance and replenishments. If implemented according to best practices[57], the net cost of biochar should be negative. In other words, the farmer's bottom line profit will increase as a result of the use of biochar soil amendments. This compares favorably with the net costs of constructed wetlands.

Be low maintenance & robust

Biochar is a very durable substance and is expected to last over a thousand years in the soil.[58] During this residence, it will continue to perform according to expectations. There are some lands in the South America where traditional char amendments are still showing positive effects hundreds of years after their original implementation.[59] As the char is gradually depleted, new influxes may be added incrementally at any time, covering any part of the area, and using any of the incorporation methods already mentioned.[60]

Remain viable during periods without fresh drainage water (dry weather)

Lack of moisture will not reduce the effectiveness of the char as it will simply remain inert until reactivated.[61]

Captured nitrates are amenable to use by growers (application to farmland)

One part of biochar's action consists of retaining nitrates in the soil so that they are available to plant roots and soil microbiota. This means that the biochar will help the soil retain nitrogen, available for plants.[62] There is no need to recover and reapply the nitrogen which does not ever run-off the soil. Growers will have to apply less nitrogen to their crops and the nitrogen they do apply will be more fully taken up by their crops.

WEAVING AN EARTH ETHIC INTO A CULTURAL FABRIC

Projects: Soundtrack for Graphic Novel Trailer
Entrepreneurial Platform(s): Graphic Novel, Kickstarter.com, Cakewalk (sequencing software)
Created: 6/1/2011

Background

As long as we environmentalists sit in our ivory research labs, prognosticating doom, it is highly unlikely that the public at large will ever take control of the issue at the necessary scale. Thus, any effort to bridge the gap between specialists and good citizens is to be commended and supported. Media of all kinds can play a primary role in this regard by exposing the issues with feeling, subtlety, and intelligence. My sister's husband, Mark Siegel, a talented graphic artist as well as book publisher, approached me about composing a trailer soundtrack for his newest graphic novel, Sailor Twain. Being a novel set on the Hudson River and in some ways celebrating the importance of nature in our lives and imaginations, I jumped at the idea and produced a short soundscape for promotional use. The clip may be heard here: https://youtu.be/fFmFKC2YOzk.

SOWING SEEDS OF CLEANTECH ENTREPRENEURISM

Projects: Verplanck Cleantech Educational Center

Entrepreneurial Platform(s): Popular Science/ Innocentive Challenge, Google Docs, Pecologix Political Ecology Blotter

Created: 6/26/2011

Background

The economic woes of small-town America are legion. Businesses collapse, young folks move out, drugs and alcohol proliferate. The cleantech movement offers a leaf of hope for this dilemma by providing the possibilities of local entrepreneurship with a global impact. This project was introduced to me by Susan Midlarsky, an educator living in Verplanck, NY, a town lying in the shadow of the Indian Point Nuclear Power Plant. Our goal was to somehow create an environmental educational program that could also lead to business development in this somewhat economically stagnant town. Susan wants to set up an environmental education center on some recently donated land and she came to me for ideas on a program for the center. My recommendations: 1) cleantech technologies for retrofitting homes: based on a tour of the town, I came up with a list of applicable technologies using the Pecologix platform, 2) Verbrick: a new industry of fly-ash brick production, based on the town's historical prominence as a brick making center and the local availability of coal-fired electric plant fly-ash, and 3) summer educational workshops for advanced teens: as an example I developed a curriculum module.

Cleantech Technologies and The Verbrick Works

BIG PICTURE

Verplanck lies just below the Indian Point Nuclear Power Plant, considered by many to be one of the most dangerously situated nukes in the country. A recent donation of land to the town presents a rare opportunity to use a portion of that parcel to showcase alternative clean and green technologies that could shepherd residents of the Hudson Valley away from nuclear power and into a newer, safer, healthier, and wealthier day. A clean tech demo and education center is proposed whose purpose is to: 1) install and test cutting edge clean building and energy technologies available to residents of Verplanck and surrounding areas, 2) educate residents of Verplanck and surrounding areas on the residential installation and usage of the technologies on display, 3) stimulate interest in local businesses producing clean and green technologies (in particular the Verbrick Factory, manufacturing recycled waste materials into standard building bricks, as a tie in to the historical brick making), and 4) sponsor projects, challenges, experiments, and environmental education for high school age students of Verplanck and surrounding areas.

GUIDING DESIGN PRINCIPLES

1) utilize local materials

2) utilize local energy sources

3) recycle local wastes into materials

4) support local manufacturers

5) reduce toxic loads

6) reduce environmental footprints

7) remain economically viable

8) remain architecturally true to local styles and traditions

9) test experimental materials and techniques

TECHNIQUES, MATERIALS, AND PRODUCTS FOR CONSIDERATION

BUILDING STRUCTURE

Poured Earth with Internal Insulation

Cast Earth

Low Carbon Cement
Pulverized Fly Ash
Magnesium Oxide
Hycrete waterproofing
PET bottle aggregate
Gypsum as solidifier
recycled concrete aggregate
hemcrete
local lime from calcium looping
brick dust waste
photocatalytic finishing
crushed oyster shell

Fluourescent Minerals

Reynobond: smog reducing aluminum

Intensive green roofing

Phase change materials for insulation

Pneumocell: inflatable building elements

Solar Roof Tiles and Shingles

EXTERIORS

Nanosurface for ice prevention on driveways, walkways

Sunagoke Moss Panels

Plastisoil for driveways and walkways

Native plants

INTERIORS

Songwood: 100% recycled wood products

Non-toxic fire retardants

Laser-cut cork, cork fabric

Sunagoke Moss Panels

Pine cone flour particle board

Recycled Glass: Ice Stone, Vetrazzo, EcoFlooring

AIR

Formaldehyde removing plants

Low VOC materials

Anti-fungal materials

WATER

PVC-free plumbing

Greywater re-use

Magnetic Ion Exchange Polymers

WASTE

Compost to Biomass Fuel

Anaerobic Digestion to Biogas

HEATING, COOLING, POWER

Radiant heat flooring

Geothermal heat pump, triple function

Biomass Furnace

Biodiesel boiler

Net Metering

12 volt wiring

12 volt appliances

Point of Use Water Heating

Propane, NG Solid Oxide Fuel Cell

SENSORS

Realtime sensory network

Litmuscreen

Salinity Front

The Challenge

Solvers are to submit an original lesson plan that meets all the requirements below. It needs to be the Solvers own work and they must have copyrights to it. The work should not have been previously published in the open literature more than 1 year ago. Work published for < 1year would be acceptable as long as the Solver still retains the copyrights to it.

The lesson plan should be appropriate for middle-school level science. As a reference, the Massachusetts Science and Technology/Engineering Curriculum Frameworkfor grades 6-8 is attached which are based on nationally recommended frameworks. This is for reference, but Solvers should incorporate some of these standards into their lesson plan to make it more valuable for educators who must cover this required material.

Any proposed solution should address the following Technical Requirements:

1. The lesson plan should be appropriate for middle school science and meet some of the Curriculum Framework standards for grades 6-8 in the attached document.

2. The lesson plan needs to cover one of the five science and technology categories below:

A. Biomimetic Design– The lesson plan should seek to both reveal and imitate the design of a naturally occurring phenomenon, such as the motion of fish fins, the resilience of wood, the human gait, or other natural mechanisms.

B. Climate Change– The lesson plan should reveal fundamental information about the nature of climate change—perhaps how it happens, how irreversible it may be, or how unforeseen consequences arise from otherwise innocuous-seeming shifts in climate. (Note: Lessons should be based on accepted scientific findings and not on any assumptions about climate change or global warming. Lessons that seek simply to prove or disprove its existence will not be appropriate for this Challenge.)

C. Fuel Cells– The lesson plan should illustrate the basic function and future potential of fuel cells, perhaps by explaining their chemical basis, their basic premise, or how they function within a larger mechanism.

D. Polymers– The lesson plan should explain the nature of new materials, perhaps by demonstrating how repeated structural units can be assembled to create a useful macromolecule.

E. "Big Data" Analysis– The lesson plan should combine sociological analysis and hard statistics to provide useful and surprising interpretations of large amounts of data. The lesson should provide a data set or point to examples that are publicly available.

3. The lesson plan should be teachable in one to three 50 minute sessions.

4. The required materials for the lesson should be readily available and not cost more than $50. You can assume a class size of 20 students.

5. The lesson plan must include a hands on activity for all students. It can include some educator demonstration activities, but it must include a "hands on" portion.

6. The lesson plan should be appropriate for 6 – 8 grade level science and should include some of the standards in the attached documents.

7. The lesson plan must be the original work of the Solver. The Solver must own the copyrights to the submission and it should not have been published in the open literature more than one year ago.

The Solution

Sketch for Lesson Plan Challenge[63]

GOAL: To create a 5 x 50 minute lesson plans covering the challenge requirements so that the five lessons form a mini-course in sustainability science and technology adaptable for use at Verplanck S&T Educational Center. Optional: Any of the lesson plans could be expanded to two or three 50 minute lessons.

JUSTIFICATION: This series weaves the topic areas into a coherent narrative starting with identification of a problem (1) and observing impacts (2), leading to technology creation system that includes the search for possible solutions (3), and the application of technology to two real-world problems: sustainable materials and energy (4 , 5).

TASKS: Susan: 1) draft lesson plans according to recognized educational standards, 2) officially register for this Innocentive challenge and list Adam as team member, 3) work with Adam on revisions, 4) submit lesson plans by October deadline. Adam: 1) prepare sketch of lesson thematic contents, 2) review and edit lesson plans, 3) draft submission text other than lesson plans, 4) provide table of references (with hyperlinks) to concepts addressed in each plan.

Challenge Topic Areas and Lesson Contents

1) Big Data: How Global Footprints Allow Us to Comprehend Humanity's Future

Precis: Students see the big picture of sustainability by working with ecological footprints of nations. Concepts: ecosystems, ecological footprint, carrying capacity, and ecological deficit. Hands On: Biological Informatics: calculation of individual footprints; comparison of national ecological footprints. Applicable Framework Standards: Life Sciences: #25, #26, #27, #28, #29

2) Climate Change: How Climate Change Affects Ecology

Precis: Students learn what climate change is and see how unsustainable behavior impacts natural world by exploring actual ecological studies. Concepts: heat transfer in Earth system, Milankovitch Cycles, biological metabolism and homeostasis, environmental factors and evolution. Hands On: Lab: experiment showing heat transfers through fluids, (local option: visit to Mohonk preserve to view annual vegetation records showing shifting dates of arrival of Spring). Applicable Framework Standards: Earth and Space Sciences #3, #4, #11; Life Sciences: #22, #25, #26, #27, #28, #29; Physical Sciences: #44, #45, #46.

3) Biomimicry: How Plant Cellulose Became Fossil Fuel Plastic

Precis: Students see how pure research and observation of nature can lead to life bettering human technologies, understand problem of fossil fuel based plastics. Concepts: conceptualize a problem, develop possible solution, and model a prototype in two dimensions. Hands On: Field Research/Secondary Research: students assigned to find something in nature and then suggest and design a human technology based on the natural phenomenon; or to bring in an example from scientific literature of biomimicry. Applicable Framework Standards: Technology/Engineering: #2.1, #2.2, #2.3, #7.2.

4) Polymers: How Bioplastics Could Replace Fossil Fuel Plastics

Precis: Students learn basic chemical theory and principles of chemical synthesis. Concepts: atomic theory, elements, compounds, physical properties of materials, biomass, waste recycling and reuse, green chemistry. Hands On: Lab: properties of biopolymers, natural polymers, and synthetic polymers. Applicable Framework Standards: Physical Sciences: #31, #32, #33, #35, #36, #37, #39.

5) Fuel Cells: How Nanopolymers Could Become an Essential Fuel Cell Technology

Precis: Students learn basics of fuel cell and understand challenges of widespread implementation of fuel cells, learn about current research using nanotechnology. Concepts: technology systems and development, communication technologies, manufacturing technologies. Hands On: Lab: build a simple fuel cell. Applicable Framework Standards: Physical Sciences: #40, #43; Technology/ Engineering: 2.6, 3.3, 4.4.

This series weaves the topic areas into a coherent narrative starting with identification of the problem (1) and observing impacts (2), leading to technology creation system that includes the search for possible solutions (3), and the application of the technology to two real-world.

ONE CHIP, ONE VOTE: VOTING FOR THE 21st CENTURY

Projects: Electronic Voting System Development

Entrepreneurial Platform(s): Yahoo Groups, Vizu.com

Created: Ongoing

Background

Recent trends around the world: the rise of authoritarian and militaristic governments, the number of contested elections and the ensuing civil unrest that often follows, the carving up of sovereignties along ethnic and sectarian lines, the difficulties of setting up functioning democracies in formerly authoritarian lands, and others, all point to a flaw in the way democracy is exercised in many places around the world. The problem is twofold: 1) the procedural mechanics of the voting leave the door open for unhappy voters to claim that the entire process was fraudulent and unfair, and 2) the system of pure plurality voting whereby each voter may choose one, and only one, option among many means that minority voters have no say in the results and therefore very little satisfaction. In places with large minority populations or many different minority populations this means an unstable democracy leading to the trends described above. So with these concerns in mind, we propose the following voting system based on free access to voting data, voter secrecy, and the range voting system of selecting the most favored candidate(s) or option(s). This system blogged to a web site dedicated to the theory of voting systems and received numerous comments. A selection of these comments, along with my responses, follows after the description.

Basic Elements For Fair and Accurate Voting

1) verification of the identity of each voter,

2) secrecy of the ballot,

3) a redundant paper record for future verification,

4) an accurate counting system that measures the voting preference so as to maximize satisfaction within the entire voting electorate,

5) a way of independently verifying each of the prior 4 elements by any voter or organization.

Proposed Solution

1) voter registration involves a biometric record for each voter (identity data base),

2) inside polling stations (or other computer for absentees), voter identification is verified using biometrics (identity verified by the system, not voting officials),

3) the voter is issued a voter serial number (the voter keeps a record of the number); a master list of voter name and serial numbers is kept, but only the numbers are to be made available to public via internet list.

4) voter places vote using an electronic system that can generate an instant paper copy of the vote bearing a random non-sequential bar code but no individual identification of any kind; the first copy is printed at the polling station for voter confirmation (the voter keeps this copy for later post-election verification of his or her vote see below); once the voter verifies the accuracy of the paper he presses a button to approve the paper version and two more copies of the document are printed instantly (bearing the same non-sequential bar code as the voter's): one goes to each of the local, state, and Federal voting commission archives (as many government branches as necessary), and others to any independent

monitoring organizations supervising the vote. These copies serve as independently verifiable, backup paper records of the election (only the voter can match his bar coded copy with the copies held by the other archives, but the archives can match bar codes against each other).

4a) As an additional safeguard, random printable facsimiles of imaginary votes are made widely available via internet and polling stations so that vote buying is impossible. The fake ballot receipts allow anyone could access to 'prove their vote' to a buyer. These fake ballots would be issued in equal quantities for all election options so as not to affect the actual vote count. The buyers would have no way of knowing if the ballot receipt was a fake or real as they would appear as real votes when looked up on the election web record of results.

5) At the moment that the vote is approved by the voter, the system assigns a vote serial number to the vote (which is not the same as the voter serial number from step 1); all of these vote serial numbers are shuffled randomly as soon after each new vote as practicable (this continuous random shuffling assures secrecy of the ballot), the system then tallies each vote using the random serial numbers as the record identifiers.

6) In elections where there are 3 or more options for a given position or referendum, then each voter votes for a first choice and additional choices: the

voter may, but is not required, to vote for each of the options. A range of values from 0 to 10 is available for each level of choice with 0 being lowest preference and 10 being the highest. The voter may assign a value to any number of the choices and may also assign equal values to different choices. The assigned values are then added up to determine the winner. This allows for a truer reflection of the will of the people than an either/or system and avoids the dilution of voting due to multiple choices. Example (9 voters, 3 choices, range is 0 to 10):

CHOICE	V1	V2	V3	V4	V5	V6	V7	V8	V9	Either/Or	Range
A	1	10	0	0	10	10	0	10	1	4	42
B	9	0	8	9	0	0	0	0	8	2	34
C	8	0	8	8	0	0	10	0	10	2	43

This example portrays a variety of voting behaviors. All the A Voters (2,5,6,8) voted strategically, giving 10 points to A and 0 points to everyone else. Voters 1 and 4 preferred B to C but cared little for A (although Voter 4 felt slightly more strongly about C . Voter 3 was undecided between B and C. Voter 7 was a strategic voter for C. Voter 9 preferred C to B slightly and cared little for A. Under the either/or system, candidate A has a strict majority with 4 top point value votes and candidates B and C are tied with 2, while under the Range Voting system, choice C wins. The amount of voter satisfaction (sum of assigned values) under the Either/Or result is 42 while under the Range Voting result the satisfaction is 43. The result of Range Voting is a choice that satisfies the wishes of the greatest number of voters.

NOTE ON STRATEGIC VOTING: Let us assume for a moment that everyone were to vote strategically (10 for their candidate and 0 for the rest), then the result is the same as regular old plurality voting like we have now in the US so this system can't be any worse than what we already have. BUT if any voters are able to assign a positive value to any choice other than their own then these secondary preferences would mean the difference between a log jam and a functioning democratic vote. The Voting Range system thus gives a meaningful voice to minority voters as well as non-strategic voters, making the overall result more satisfactory to the whole population. From what I have been told by voting scientists, the Range Voting system can be implemented using existing voting machine software without major modification.

7) Post-election, the following data is on internet: 1) the complete list of voter serial numbers (but no names) so every voter may make sure their number is on the list and see the total number of voters, 2) voting results for each candidate and measure on the ballot identified by bar code (same bar code that was printed on the printed paper documents), so anyone can view their own voting results by bar code (since

only the voter know his or her bar code then secrecy is maintained).

8) Range voting is also applicable to legislative voting except that the legislation should be broken into constituent parts so that each legislator may cast a vote on each sub-unit. The reason for this is that it is very hard to vote simply yea or nay on 500 page legislation covering all kinds of disparate subjects. Supposing the bill consists of 10 titles with each title having 10 chapters and each chapter having 10 sections and each chapter 10 sub-sections, down to the smallest unit of the bill. Each legislator could cast a range vote for each and every part at his or her own discretion. One legislator could vote 10 for the entire bill at once (thereby giving 10 points to each sub-unit down to the smallest), while another might choose to vote by title, and another by the smallest unit of the bill. In the end, one would have a law, each constituent part of which satisfies the greatest number of legislators while avoiding the problem of strategic legislation that seeks to foist pork-barrel legislation on the whole by attaching these types of provisions to ones that seek to attain a more general public good.

Comments and Questions by Bloggers

QUESTION: How does the average person verify that the fake votes have not affected the vote tallies, without knowing which votes are real and which ones are fake?

SIMILAR QUESTION: Can the vote buyers and coercers see the list of counted votes and then compare if the bought/coerced vote was real or not?

SIMILAR QUESTION: Can the coercer/buyer check if the ballot (of someone else) that he has received is valid?

RESPONSE: At the end of the election that results would show the total number of voters (using the initial voter serials issued upon entering the voting booth), how each of these voters voted (using the randomized serials issued after the vote on the voting booth screen had been confirmed by the voter), and also the total vote counts (including fake votes). So if there were 3 voters, for example: the result tables would show that random serial #1 voted for A, random #2 for B, and random #3 for B and that 3 actual voters voted. The total tally though would show that A received 11 and B 12 votes due to 10 fake votes issued to each of the candidates. In other words, you know the total number of actual votes and how they voted AND you know the total number of votes counted so you can easily see how many fake votes were attributed to each candidate. This would be verifiable by the open cross checks and individual voter policing permitted by the voting system (i.e., using the voting receipts that had been printed out to the varying authorities and observers as well as by any individual voter confirmations). Now supposing some one who wanted to buy A's vote tries to confirm the vote receipt given to him by A. He will upload the bar code (or other form of graphic coding) and the system will respond that this vote was received and counted for candidate B, but will not say whether this was a real or fake ballot. The system would not allow general users to associate a scanned-in paper receipt with a random serial# (only to verify how the vote was counted), although this information would be available to the independent observers and the voting authorities as well as the voter in the case of a voter alleging some kind of error.

BLOG COMMENT: Quite interesting and also simple approach. I think I should be able to print myself both real and imaginary votes at the voting location to be able to fool the one that told (coerced) me to vote certain way or the one that wants to buy my vote. This system would make it possible to check and complain if my vote is not counted but this would allow also false claims of non-counted votes. There is also a risk that the machine gives the same code to several voters that vote the same way (do you trust the machine or not).

RESPONSE: I don't think you'd be able to print more then one receipt of the vote at the ballot box (the voting terminals would be very simple devices with no control ability and remember that every receipt is printed at two other places: the voting authority and the independent verifier as well as given a randomized serial number; if the total number of randomized serials did not match the actual number of serialized voters, see above for details on serialization, then there would have to be a procedure for declaring part or all of the voting void: that is the point of the system to catch irregularities).

FOLLOW UP: I was worried about cases where 1) I can't get the kind of copy that my coercer told me to vote and 2) someone can buy votes since voters can with reasonable probability demonstrate that they voted as agreed (since getting a similar copy is improbable).

RESPONSE: There would be plenty of fake ballot receipts available for every candidate or option. The widely available fake ballot receipts would be identical to real receipts. Only the data base could verify which were which. There would be issued equal numbers of fake ballot receipts that looked just like the real thing (but of course were bar coded as fake in the system) that would make it impossible for vote buyers or coercers to know if they represented a live vote or not.

QUESTION: What if the party that lost the election presents a high number of imaginary votes that can not be found on the list and claims that they are real votes?

RESPONSE: Remember that each vote, real and fake, is simultaneously printed to each of the government voting commissions (at every level necessary, local, state, federal) and to NGO observers. That means that every vote is on a number of lists. If someone brings in a ballot receipt that is note found in any of the other receipt archives then that ballot is a counterfeit (as opposed to an official fake). If that ballot receipt is found in other archives but not on the computer data base then there has been an error and the review process would need to determine how best to respond. Perhaps the best way would be to set up a day when voters whose ballots had been miscounted could re-vote the same way as above and a new tally could be calculated.

I don't see how there would be false claims of non-counted votes. The system maintains a web open list of coded votes and the results of these votes so that any voter could see whether their coded vote is in the system (and count all the votes if desired). If their ballot receipt code does not appear in the system then this could be checked easily as follows: the voter, still anonymously on a voting authority web page, triggers an inquiry and uploads a scan of his or her ballot. The voting authority and independent agency must then upload their copy of the ballot corresponding to the bar code. If they match then we know the ballot is real and can then proceed to confirm that this bar coded vote appears on the web accessible voting record list. If not then it is entered by the voting authority. To avoid abuse, a fee system could be instituted for unfounded claims.

BLOGGER: I'm not quite sure which parts of the system were assumed to always work properly and where the foul play was expected to emerge. If the (networked) machines are always right they could just count the (correct) results and be done with it. If the machines and data in the machines could be manipulated then new risks emerge. As for machine error, nothing is presumed. This is why we maintain the computer data base AND a multiple and identical paper record that is verified by the voter at the moment of voting. It would be fairly easy for the system itself to continuously check if there were duplicate bar codings issued and flag any errors immediately. The point of all this is to create a system that everyone can verify (open) and that can be used to detect errors (redundancy of paper records to independent verifiers).

BLOGGER: Duplicate bar codes could be misused e.g. so that the (rigged) machine would give the same bar code to two voters that vote the same way. Then the machine would add one vote to keep the number of votes correct. The new vote would be according to the preferences of the person that rigged the machine.

RESPONSE: This is overcome by the simultaneous printing of ballot receipts to multiple locations. The command to print at the polling station would be the same command (in series) going to all the other locations so that it is physically impossible to print at one location but not the others. True, different voters who voted the same way would never know that they received the same graphic coding. But since each receipt printed to voters is also printed to the multiple locations, they would each be able to compare their own receipts for duplication of coding. Furthermore, there would have to be an extra ballot printed (the stuffed ballot) going to each of the multiple locations and this extra ballot would unbalance the number of votes versus number of voters at the satellite locations. Another potential rigging would be that somehow a voting machine was able to simply invent voters and print these ballots to the multiple locations only. Since the voting machines are independent systems from the voter serial machines, there would be no way for the voting machine to alter the number of voters to match the number of votes. So the safety is achieved by separation of computing systems and by the mechanical serialization of printing commands (not software mediated) so that any given print command must be executed at each printing location.

ABOUT THE AUTHOR

Adam D. Carfagno Cherson is an International Ecological Policy Attorney. From 2006 until 2015 he edited *Ecosider* (ecosider.wordpress.com). In 2006, he co-authored the white paper "Addressing Electronic Waste in New York City" for the Natural Resources Defense Council. His book review of "An Ocean Blueprint for the 21st Century" appeared in Columbia's Journal of International Affairs in 2005. From 2006 to 2007 he was a member of the International Environmental Law Committee of the Association of the Bar of the City of New York. In 2007, he was a member of the Reef Educational Foundation scuba team that surveyed the Flower Garden Banks in the Gulf of Mexico as part of a NOAA expedition to the area. His article *"Rapid Site Selection and Performance Measurement of Marine Reserves...,"* published on Reefbase.org, applies GIS modeling and Landsat satellite imagery to the largest known database of Caribbean fish species sightings. He is a photographic contributor to Fishbase.org, an international ichthyological database developed by the World Fish Center and the Food and Agriculture Organization of the United Nations. He holds an AB from Harvard University, a JD from Tulane Law School, and an MPA in Environmental Science and Policy from Columbia University.

END NOTES

[1] Submitted to various venture capital firms.

[2] This letter accompanied an earlier version of the project concept. Some of the technical and economic details have changed. The most current version of the concept is presented in the next sub-section (Innocentive Challenge). This letter is included here due to its exposition of important explanatory material.

[3] http://www.nycbar.org/pdf/report/uploads/20072035-ReporttotheMayorsOfficeReNewYorkCitysEnergyPlanPlaNYC2030.pdf

[4] New York State Energy Planning Board, New York State Energy Plan 2009, Climate Change Issue Brief, p.24, http://www.nysenergyplan.com/final/Climate_Change_IB.pdf

[5] Bioenergy Feedstock Information Network, Biomass Resources, Oak Ridge National Laboratory, http://bioenergy.ornl.gov/main.aspx

[6] U.S. Department of Labor, Bureau of Labor Statistics, Average Energy Prices in New York-Northern New Jersey, October 2010, http://www.bls.gov/ro2/avgengny.pdf

[7] New York State Energy Planning Board, Renewable Energy Assessment, 2009: "Renewable electricity resources reduce the net retail price of electricity paid by all ratepayers...", p. 2, http://www.nysenergyplan.com/final/Renewable_Energy_Assessment.pdf

[8] http://politicalecology.xyvy.info/fossil-fuel-subsidies-are-12-times-support-for-renewables/

[9] U.S. Department of Energy, Property-Assessed Clean Energy (PACE) Programs, http://www1.eere.energy.gov/wip/solutioncenter/financialproducts/pace.html

[10] In an energy aligned lease a landlord is permitted to amortize the costs of making energy efficiency upgrades and to pass those costs through to the tenant to the extent of the tenant's new energy savings.

[11] Palmujoki, et al. Green Public Procurement: Environmental Criteria Found in RFP Often Lacking in Subsequent Contracts. RECIEL, October 6, 2010. http://dx.doi.org/10.1111/j.1467-9388.2010.00681.x

[12] Biodiesel from Sewage Sludge: http://dx.doi.org/10.1021/ef1001106; ; Non-recyclable Plastics and Rubbers: http://dx.doi.org/10.1039/b908135f ; Plasma Vitrification: http://dx.doi.org/10.1021/es101244u; Liquid Fuels: http://dx.doi.org/10.1016/j.energy.2010.04.048; Microbial Fuel Cells: http://dx.doi.org/10.1021/es100125h; Anaerobic Digestion: http://dx.doi.org/10.1016/j.scitotenv.2009.10.072; Biofuels and District Heat: http://dx.doi.org/10.1016/j.enpol.2009.07.071; Hydrogen: ttp://dx.doi.org/10.1021/ie100620e; Biogas: http://dx.doi.org/10.1016/j.wasman.2010.04.011; Dimethyl Ether: http://dx.doi.org/10.1007/s11708-010-0121-y

[13] U.S. Department of Energy, Alternative Fueling Stations, http://www.afdc.energy.gov/afdc/fuels/stations.html

[14] US Environmental Protection Agency, Diesel School Buses, http://cfpub.epa.gov/schools/top_sub.cfm?t_id=37&s_id=38

[15] Public Participation in Environmental Assessment and Decision Making: National Research Council: http://www.nap.edu/catalog.php?record_id=12434

[16] http://dx.doi.org/10.1111/j.1365-2664.2010.01874.x

[17] http://dx.doi.org/10.1021/es802119h

[18] http://www.carbontrust.co.uk/Publications/pages/publicationdetail.aspx?id=CTG020&respos=1&q=asphalt&o=Rank&od=asc&pn=0&ps=10

[19]http://www.www.eapa.org/usr_img/position_paper/fuel_efficiency_report.pdf, p.15.

[20] http://www.nytimes.com/2007/11/26/us/26chicago.html?_r=1

[21] http://dx.doi.org/10.1021/es802119h

[22] http://dx.doi.org/10.1088/1748-9326/5/1/014005

[23] http://www.greenroads.us and http://www.rmrc.unh.edu

[24] http://www.nyc.gov/html/nycwasteless/downloads/pdf/wp-reports/wprr06.pdf

[25] http://www.npr.org/templates/story/story.php?storyId=113969321

[26] Urban Green Council, Cost of Green in NYC, October 1, 2009, http://www.urbangreencouncil.org/advocacy/coststudy/

[27] Rosenthal, Elisabeth, "Europe Finds Clean Energy in Trash, but U.S. Lags", New York Times, April 12, 2010.

[28] Yan, S. et al., Emerging Contaminants of Environmental Concern: Source, Transport, Fate, and Treatment. Pract. Periodical of Haz., Toxic, and Radioactive Waste Mgmt. Volume 14, Issue 1, pp. 2-20 (January 2010). DOI: 10.1061/(ASCE)HZ.1944-8376.0000015

[29] Brooks, B. et al. Determination of select antidepressants in fish from an effluent-dominated stream. Environmental Toxicology and Chemistry, 24: 464–469 (2005). DOI: 10.1897/04-081R.1; Ramirez, AJ, et al. Occurrence of pharmaceuticals and personal care products in fish: Results of a national pilot study in the united states. Environmental Toxicology and Chemistry, 28: 2587–2597 (2009). DOI:

10.1897/08-561.1; Kumar, A. and Xagoraraki, I. Pharmaceuticals, personal care products and endocrine-disrupting chemicals in U.S. surface and finished drinking waters: A proposed ranking system. Science of The Total Environment Volume 408, Issue 23, 1 November 2010, Pages 5972-5989. DOI: 10.1016/j.scitotenv.2010.08.048

[30] Sabourin, L. et al. Runoff of pharmaceuticals and personal care products following application of dewatered municipal biosolids to an agricultural field. Science of The Total Environment Volume 407, Issue 16, 1 August 2009, Pages 4596-4604. DOI:10.1016/j.scitotenv.2009.04.027

[31] Ort, Christopher, et al. Sampling for Pharmaceuticals and Personal Care Products (PPCPs) and Illicit Drugs in Wastewater Systems: Are Your Conclusions Valid? A Critical Review. Environ. Sci. Technol., 2010, 44 (16), pp 6024–6035. DOI: 10.1021/es100779n

[32] Perez, G. et al. Electro-oxidation of reverse osmosis concentrates generated in tertiary water treatment. Water Research Volume 44, Issue 9, May 2010, Pages 2763-2772. DOI: 10.1016/j.watres.2010.02.017

[33]http://www.columbia.edu/cu/mpaenvironment/pages/projects/sum2005/Marine%20Debris%20Final%20Report%20Sum2005.pdf

[34] Abstract Submitted to the 5th International Marine Debris Conference

[35] This is a summary for purposes of team formation.

[36] Other fastener systems such as stitching, zip-lock, or zippering, may be substituted for hook-and-fastener tape.

[37]In every case, the release altitude of each individual container is fully configurable according to mission demands.

[38]Please see Appendix of Calculations.

[39] The release altitude of each container is fully configurable according to mission demands.

[40] The roller conveyor specifications are subject to modification.

[41] The release altitude of each individual container is fully configurable according to mission demands.

[42] Due to the unavailability of a schematic diagram of the C-130 cargo area floor these unit needs are estimated. The actual number, dimensions, and type of heavy roller modules could vary somewhat based on the actual demands of the C-130 cargo floor.

[43] Assumes 50 missions per year for 10 years; each mission drops 22,400 lbs. of food and water.

[44] Complete data, indices, formulas, and statistical results underlying this solution may be found in the supplementary materials

[45] Normality, linearity, outliers, multicollinearity, and heteroskedasticity; need for variable transformation also assessed

[46] See e.g., Lee, James W, et al.. 2010. Characterization of Biochars Produced from Cornstovers for Soil Amendment, Environ. Sci. Technol. 44 (20), pp 7970–7974. doi: 10.1021/es101337x

[47] A biochar pyrolysis reactor is a fairly simple piece of light industrial equipment. One such model is being developed by Biochar Solutions: http://www.biocharsolutions.com/technology/index.html

[48] Harley, Andrew. 2010. The role of biochar in the carbon dynamics of drastically disturbed soils. In 'U.S.-Focused Biochar Report: Assessment of Biochar's Benefits for the United States'. (Ed. Jonah Levine), Table 1, p. 28 (Center for Energy and Environmental Security: Boulder,

Colorado).http://www.biochar-us.org/pdf%20files/biochar_report_lowres.pdf

[49] Steiner, Christoph. 2010. Biochar from agricultural and forestry residues – a complimentary use of "Waste" Biomass. In 'U.S.-Focused Biochar Report: Assessment of Biochar's Benefits for the United States'. (Ed. Jonah Levine), pp. 1-14 (Center for Energy and Environmental Security: Boulder, Colorado). http://www.biochar-us.org/pdf%20files/biochar_report_lowres.pdf

[50] Knowles, OA, et al. Biochar for the mitigation of nitrate leaching from soil amended with biosolids. 2011. Science of The Total Environment, Volume 409, Issue 17, Pages 3206-3210. doi:10.1016/j.scitotenv; also mentioned in Harley (2010).

[51] Major J, et al. 2009. Biochar Effects on Nutrient Leaching. In 'Biochar for Environmental Management: Science and Technology'. (Eds J Lehmann and S Joseph) pp. 271-287. (Eartscan: London), cited in Harley (2010).

[52] McLaughlin, Hugh. 2010. Biochar and Energy Co-Products. In 'U.S.-Focused Biochar Report: Assessment of Biochar's Benefits for the United States'. (Ed. Jonah Levine), pp. 15-26 (Center for Energy and Environmental Security: Boulder, Colorado). http://www.biochar-us.org/pdf%20files/biochar_report_lowres.pdf

[53] Mukherjeea, AR, et al. 2011. Surface chemistry variations among a series of laboratory-produced biochars, Geoderma, Volume 163, Issues 3-4, Pages 247-255. doi:10.1016/j.geoderma.2011.04.021

[54] Major, Julie. 2010. Guidelines on Practical Aspects of Biochar Application to Field Soil in Various Soil Management Systems. (International Biochar Initiative: Westerville, Ohio)http://www.biochar-international.org/sites/default/files/IBI%20Biochar%20Application%20Guidelines_web.pdf

[55] Spokas, KA. 2010. Review of the stability of biochar in soils: predictability of O:C molar ratios. Carbon Management, Vol. 1, No. 2, Pages 289-303. doi: 10.4155/cmt.10.32

[56] Op. cit., Knowles (2011).

[57] Op. cit., Major (2010).

[58] Op. cit., Spokas (2010).

[59] Lehmann, J, et al. 2003. Nutrient availability and leaching in an archaeological Anthrosol and a Ferralsol of the Central Amazon basin: fertilizer, manure and charcoal amendments. Plant and Soil, 249:343-357.

[60] Op. cit., Major (2010).

[61] Op. cit., Lehmann (2003).

[62] Steiner, C, et al. 2008. Nitrogen Retention and Plant Uptake on a Highly Weathered Central Amazonian Ferralsol amended with Compost and Charcoal. Journal of Plant Nutrition and Soil Science, Volume 171, Issue 6, pages 893–899. doi: 10.1002/jpln.200625199

[63] This solution was never completed for submission to Innocentive.

www.ingramcontent.com/pod-product-compliance
Lightning Source LLC
Chambersburg PA
CBHW020858180526
45163CB00007B/2547
* 9 7 8 1 5 2 0 6 3 3 9 2 3 *